# BAKER'S "FLOWER"

## Quick-Mix Cookbook

# BAKER'S "FLOWER"

## Quick-Mix Cookbook

**KAYE MANNING**

Illustrated by
**H. K. MANNING**

Betterway Publications, Inc.
White Hall, Virginia

First Printing:

Published by Betterway Publications, Inc.
White Hall, VA 22987

Book design by Diane Nelson
Illustrations by H. K. Manning
Calligraphy by Rosamond Casey

**Library of Congress Cataloging in Publication Data**

Manning, Kaye,
    The baker's "flower" quick mix cookbook.

    Includes index.
    1. Cookery.   I. Title.
TX715.M2845   1985         641.5'55         84–28232
ISBN 0-932620-42-6 (pbk.)

Printed in the United States of America

# Table of Contents

This book is dedicated with love and special thanks to my three daughters — Trace, for testing foods while she was away at school — H.K. for her beautiful artwork, and to Meg who ate lots of cookies.

Many thanks to all of the people who helped me directly and indirectly. I could not have accomplished the writing of this book without the wide variety of wonderful cookbooks and magazines which I used for references, resource material, and creative inspiration.

Many of my questions were answered in the TASTE food section of the Minneapolis Star and Tribune by restaurants and individuals who contributed special recipes, tips, and other information.

My subscriptions to Food and Wine, Sunset, and Cuisine magazines brought an insight into trends, techniques, and recipes which were incorporated with my ideas.

Also, special thanks to those who helped me by testing recipes and for being encouraging and supportive. And, for all of those who contributed suggestions and advice, I am truly grateful.

I tried to find all answers to everything. Of course, I eventually discovered that was impossible. What I ended up doing was to include pertinent information for ingredients and equipment with a particular recipe, or, in conjunction with several recipes.

This has been written in so many different stages that sometimes even my methods changed. I've tried to re-do and make everything as consistent as possible — but, there comes a point when . . .

# Introduction

Writing this book has been an uphill battle with small failures and great successes!

Four years ago, I decided to write a cookbook. My goal was to put together a collection of updated traditional foods. As I was compiling data, I came across recipes I'd saved on making home mixes. I got caught up with the notion that I could make many of my targeted recipes from no more than three basic home mixes. With that idea, I created a biscuit mix, a cake mix, and a pudding mix. Later, after much testing, I realized that with some minor changes, the three could be combined into one single mix.

One of the greatest challenges was naming the mix. Because of baking so many breads, cakes and cookies, I thought of it as a bakery mix. Therefore, the Baker's part of the name seemed very appropriate. After searching through the thesaurus and unabridged dictionary, I discovered that flower is really the predecessor of the word flour. Flour has taken on a different significance along with the change in spelling. The old French word "fleur" refers to the flowering part of the grain stalks. Webster's dictionary describes "flower" as the best or finest part of a thing. Baker's "Flower" seemed the perfect word combination to describe the product.

In recent years, we have developed an increasing awareness about nutrition. We have become concerned about what goes into our bodies and our children's bodies. At the same time, we have many more working people who have less time for cooking and baking and are forced to buy convenience type foods. With this mix, good cooking does not have to be sacrificed. Recipes were written to eliminate unnecessary steps and ingredients and still provide some personal options. The recipes are basic and very usable by new cooks, and at the same time, will be equally at home in the kitchen of accomplished cooks who have other interests and are looking for easier methods of making traditional recipes.

I fear that cooking is another fading art. It _is_ time consuming and many recipes are so poorly written that wasting time, money, and energy in the kitchen simply cannot be justified. I have rewritten cooking and baking by simplifying directions, ingredients, and organization of material. I've tried to build in options and keep ingredients and cooking equipment to a minimum.

I hope you'll enjoy the mix and recipes as much as I do.

Most sincerely,

Kaye Manning

# Welcome to a New Frontier in Cooking & Baking

This exciting new mix called Baker's "Flower" was designed for today's cook. It is a convenience food, yet true to tradition, it bakes the old-fashioned way.

The all-purpose mix is made with simple ingredients from your kitchen cupboard, blended together with a pastry cutter to form a "dry" mix. This mix can be stored in a tightly closed container on your kitchen shelf for up to 6 weeks.

You'll love the simple, dependable recipes. Newer cooks will enjoy recipes for the latest trends in foods, the few ingredients required, and the easy-to-follow directions. Experienced cooks will appreciate the variety of traditional foods made easier with the time-saving mix and concise recipes.

In many of the recipes, Baker's "Flower" is the primary ingredient. Other recipes may require a small amount but it is, nevertheless, an important contributing factor to the final food product. Extra recipes have been included which do <u>not</u> require Baker's "Flower" — these have been added to facilitate you in total food preparation.

A great advantage to the mix is that once it's made, there's no more messy measuring from the can of solid vegetable shortening. Extra shortening additions are all made from butter, margarine, or oil.

My goal was to simplify life, not only for myself, but for you, too. You'll also discover that everything is made with the most basic equipment.

Here's wishing you the adventuresome spirit of the long ago pioneers as you travel new frontiers in your own kitchen. Happy Cooking!

# Making the Mix

You'll need the following equipment:

1. A very large bowl (5 quart size)
2. Pastry blender
3. Dry measuring cups (the nested kind)
4. Measuring spoons
5. A large mixing spoon
6. A straight-edged spatula or knife

The over-sized bowl will allow extra space for blending the dry ingredients and for cutting in the shortening.

Remember to spoon the flour into a dry measuring cup. Then, level it with a straight-edged spatula or knife.

If you're fortunate enough to own a <u>Kitchen scale</u>, you can save much time by weighing the flour and shortening.

# Baker's "Flower" ♥ All-Purpose Mix

4 c (16 oz) unbleached enriched all-purpose flour
4 c (15 oz) cake flour
1/4 c sugar
3 Tbsp baking powder
1 Tbsp salt

Weigh or measure dry ingredients into very large mixing bowl. <u>Stir</u>, or sift, until thoroughly blended.

1 1/4 c (8 oz) solid vegetable shortening — Add to dry mixture, Cut in with pastry blender until grainy.

Store in a tightly covered container in a dry, cool place in your kitchen cupboard.

Makes 10 cups

(Use within 6 weeks)

# Pertinent Notes About the Recipes and Mix

The ♥ lets you know at a glance how much Baker's "flower" will be needed for each recipe.

Spoon both flour and Baker's "flower" into measuring cups. Flours have a tendency to pack down. Level with a straight-edged knife.

Flour refers to the all-purpose kind.

Whole milk was used to test the recipes. Substituting skim milk could affect the cakes.

Large eggs were used for testing. The size of the egg will have a direct influence on the outcome of the recipe.

When using margarine, choose a good grade. Be sure to use stick, not whipped.

Where sugar is called for, use granulated. If it says brown sugar, pack it into the measuring cup. It should hold its shape when unmolded.

Use unsweetened cocoa, not the instant mix.

Oats, quick oats, dry oats, rolled oats etc. all refer to uncooked dry oatmeal.

Ingredients in parenthesis suggests that they are optional additions. An exception to this is the (flour for kneading) which just denotes an estimated guess. Also, a parenthesis sign may be used just to impart a little information (you'll know the difference).

Always read through the recipe to make sure you have all ingredients before you start.

Check to see if the oven needs preheating.

If you make the mix and then find yourself leaving for Europe, just store in a moisture-proof container in refrigerator or freezer. Be sure to bring it to room temperature before using.

# Comments from "Testers"

The OLD-FASHIONED BISCUITS are the best I've made in years.

I usually adjust amounts of ingredients when baking, but found it unnecessary with this mix. The recipes had perfect proportions.

A superb cheesecake! Best taste and texture of any recipe I've tried.

The best BANANA BREAD ever!

My favorite recipe is for the Whole Wheat Bread. It is easy to make and has the most enjoyable taste of any bread I've ever made from scratch.

With Baker's "Flower", I can make Hot Fudge Sundaes to equal the best in town.

After years of recipe searching, I could finally make Apple Crisp as good as I remember my moms.

The Bakery Cinnamon Rolls are almost like store-bought, but better.

My husband's comment was that I would never make a pie crust until now. The Baker's "Flower" recipe is as good and easy as it says.

The peanut butter cookies are the best our family has had.

The Oven-fried chicken is about as close to pan-fried as you can get.

We loved the Easy-Mix Pizza Crust.

Wonderful Brownies. Terrific Coffeecake.

I just tried the Toffee Bars - they were great!

Many thanks to Rita Bond, IND - Carolyn Younger, MN - Diane Gallivan, MN - Marty Jacobsen, MN - Donna Smith, FLA - and to all my relatives and other friends who tried my Baker's "Flower" mix.

Quick Breads

# Quick Breads · Categories & Tips

The term "Quick Breads" denotes a wide variety of food products which are cooked or baked in many different ways. They are all grouped together because they are made with quick-acting leavening (baking powder and/or baking soda) instead of the more slowly acting yeast.

They include the following categories:

## BISCUITS, TARTS, SCONES

Stir just till dough follows fork around bowl. Form into a ball on a lightly floured board. To knead, fold dough over and press with heel of hand. Bake in middle of a pre-heated oven. Best when eaten fresh and hot from the oven.

## MUFFINS

Stir just till dry ingredients are moistened. Fill greased (or paper-lined) muffin cups 2/3 full. Bake in middle of a pre-heated oven.

## PANCAKES

Pour batter onto hot, greased griddle. One of the secrets of good pancakes is having the griddle at the right temperature. To test, sprinkle with a few drops of water. If the water evaporates immediately, the griddle is too hot. If the water just stands or boils slowly, it's not hot enough. When the drops of water dance and skitter before they disappear, the griddle is ready to use. Be sure to maintain a steady temperature. Turn when puffed and full of bubbles. Brown second side — it should take about half the time of the first side.

# WAFFLES

Pour batter onto center of hot (greased if necessary) waffle iron. Bake as the manufacturer of your waffle maker directs— usually about 5 min..or until steaming stops. If waffle resists when cover is lifted, close and bake a little longer. Lift off with a fork.

# DOUGHNUTS

Chill dough for easier shaping and to reduce amount of flour needed when rolling. After cutting, let dough rest for about 20 min, uncovered. The drying helps reduce fat absorption. Fry with dried side down first. Fat temperature should be around 375°. Don't skimp on grease and don't crowd. Turn when browned on the first side. Drain on cooling rack set over paper toweling or put directly onto brown paper.

# COFFEE CAKE

Make topping first. Put batter into greased and floured pan. Sprinkle with topping. Bake in middle of pre-heated oven.

# NUT BREADS

After baking, let set 8-10 min before removing from pan to cooling rack. These slice best when cooled first. Cool completely before wrapping. For longer keeping, wrap tightly in foil and refrigerate. For a shape variation, bake in greased and floured cans. Do not fill more than 3/4 full.

For CORNBREAD, DUMPLINGS, FLOUR TORTILLAS, see MAIN DISH section. For SHORTCAKES and FRUIT COBBLERS, see OTHER DESSERTS section.

# Old-Fashioned Biscuits

450°

2 1/4 c Baker's "Flower" ♥ - Measure into
                       mixing bowl.

1/2 c milk - Add milk all at once. Stir
             quickly just till dough follows
             fork around the bowl. The
             dough will be soft, not stiff.

Turn onto a lightly floured board. Knead
10-12 turns.

Roll or pat 1/2" thick on a lightly floured
board. Cut with a 2" or 2 1/2" biscuit cutter
which has been dipped in flour.

Place on ungreased baking sheet.

Bake 450° (middle oven rack) 8-10 min.

                          8-10 biscuits

# Buttermilk Biscuits

2 1/2 c Baker's "Flower" ♥ } Stir to blend in
1/2 tsp baking soda       } mixing bowl.

2/3 c buttermilk - Add buttermilk. Mix, cut,
                and bake as for the
                OLD-FASHIONED BISCUITS.

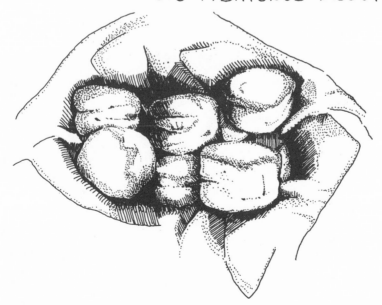

# Jam Tarts

425°

2 1/4 c Baker's "Flower" ❤ } Stir to blend
2 Tbsp sugar                  } in mixing bowl

1/4 c milk            } Add to dry ingredients.
1/4 c butter or      } Stir just till dough
  margarine, melted  } forms and leaves sides
                       of bowl.

Knead 10-12 turns on a lightly floured
board. Roll to about 1/2" thick.

Cut into 6 shortcakes — 3" diameter.

Place on ungreased baking sheet. Press a
deep indentation in each but leave a half-
inch ridge around the edge.

Fill with jam, preserves, or canned fruit
pie fillings.

Bake 425° (middle oven rack) 10 min or
until lightly browned.

# Scones

## (an English Biscuit)

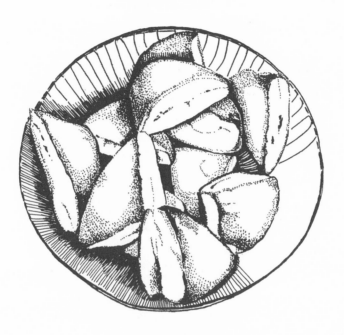

425°

2 1/3 c Baker's "Flower" ♥ } Measure into mixing
2 Tbsp sugar } bowl. Stir to blend.

1 egg, slightly beaten } Remove 1 Tbsp egg and
 (reserve 1 tbsp) } set aside. Stir remainder
1/3 c milk or cream } of egg with milk. Add to
 } dry ingredients.
Stir just to mix. Gather into a ball.
Knead on a lightly floured board about 12 turns.
Shape into a flattened rectangle. Roll to 3/8" thick
Cut into triangle shapes. Place on ungreased
baking sheet.
Brush with reserved egg. Sprinkle lightly with
sugar, if desired.

Bake 425° about 10 min or until golden brown.

# Plain Muffins

400°

2½ c Baker's "Flower" ♥ } Blend in mixing bowl.
2 Tbsp sugar

1 egg, slightly beaten } Mix together. Add all at
3/4 c milk                        once to dry ingredients.
                                        stir just to moisten. (Batter
                                        will be grainy)
spoon or use an ice cream scoop to drop
batter into greased or paper-lined muffin tins.
Bake 400° 18-20 min

Makes 10-12 muffins

# Cranberry Muffins

Follow recipe for PLAIN MUFFINS except add
1 c halved cranberries and ½ tsp orange
extract with the egg and milk addition.

sprinkle tops with sugar before baking.

# Buttermilk Muffins

Add ¼ tsp baking soda with dry ingredients.
Replace milk with 1 c buttermilk.

# Blueberry Muffins

400°

2 1/2 c Baker's "Flower" ♥ } Measure into mixing
1/3 c sugar } bowl. Stir to blend.

1 egg } Beat egg and milk together. Add
3/4 c milk } to dry ingredients. Stir just till
           blended. Batter will be grainy.

1 c fresh blueberries - Fold blueberries into
                       the batter.

Fill greased or paper-lined muffin cups
2/3 full.

Bake 400° - 20 min or until golden.

                Makes 1 doz.

# Sugar 'n Spice Mini-Muffins

375°

2 1/4 c Baker's "Flower" ❤
1/4 c sugar
1/4 tsp nutmeg
} Measure into mixing bowl. Stir to blend.

1 egg, beaten
1/2 c milk
} Add to dry ingredients. Stir till moistened.

Drop by teaspoonfuls into greased miniature muffin tins. Fill each about 2/3 full.

Bake 375° 15-20 min or until lightly browned.

Remove from pans.

1/3 c melted butter - Roll each muffin in melted butter.
3/4 c sugar
1 1/2 tsp cinnamon
} Then, roll in sugar-cinnamon mixture.

Serve hot or cold.        2-2 1/2 doz.

# Cream Cheese Clafouti

(a dessert-type pancake baked in the oven)

1 - 8 oz pkg cream cheese, softened
¼ c butter or margarine, softened
} Put into a mixing bowl. Beat with a spoon until light and fluffy.

⅓ c Baker's "Flower" ♥
⅓ c sugar
} Add to the cream cheese mixture. Beat until smooth.

½ c light cream  - Stir in gradually.

3 eggs · Add 1 at a time. Beat well after each addition.

1 - 16 oz can dark sweet pitted cherries
        or
1 - 16 oz can sliced peaches
} Drain the fruit thoroughly. If using peaches, cut into smaller pieces. Place fruit pieces in a buttered 13 x 9 baking dish.

Pour batter over the fruit.

Bake 400° 25-35 min or until golden brown. Center will be soft set. Cool slightly.

Sprinkle with powdered sugar. Let stand for 15 min before serving.

# Pancakes

1 egg  -  Beat egg in a mixing bowl.

1 c milk - Add milk; blend together.

1 2/3 c Baker's "Flower" ♥ - Add to the egg-
milk mixture.
Blend well. Batter
will be slightly grainy.

Let batter stand while griddle heats.

Fry on a <u>hot</u> greased griddle. To test for
perfect frying temperature, sprinkle surface of
griddle with a few drops of water. If they
bounce, sputter, and disappear, it's ready to use!

For a 4" pancake, use about 3 Tbsp batter —
a little less than a 1/4 c measure.

Turn when edges are dry and top has bubbled.
Flip and cook the unbaked side.

Makes 12 - 4" pancakes

Variations:

BLUEBERRY PANCAKES - Add 1/2 c fresh blueberries to the basic pancake batter.

BUTTERMILK PANCAKES- Replace milk with
1 1/4 c buttermilk. Add 1/2 tsp baking soda
with the ♥.

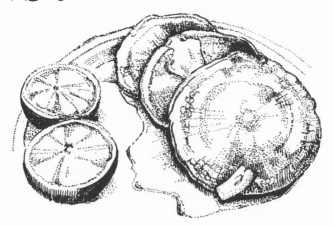

# Syrups for Pancakes

**SUGAR SYRUP —**

1 c sugar
1 c brown sugar, packed
1 c water
(vanilla)

⎫ Stir together in a saucepan. Cook and stir over med-high heat until <u>sugars</u> <u>dissolve</u>. Continue boiling slowly until of desired consistency.

(The syrup will thicken as it cools) Add flavoring to taste after removing from heat.

**MAPLE FLAVORED SYRUP —**

1 c light corn syrup
½ c brown sugar
½ c water

⎫ Combine in a saucepan. Stir until sugar is dissolved. Then, simmer for 5 min. Remove from heat.

1 Tbsp butter or margarine
Maple flavoring to taste

⎫ Add. Blend.

**STRAWBERRY SYRUP -**

1 - 10 oz pkg frozen sliced strawberries

- Thaw. Mash or blend until smooth.

½ c light corn syrup

- Combine with strawberries in a saucepan. Boil about 5 min or until syrup consistency.

**ORANGE MARMALADE SYRUP.**

3/4 c marmalade
3/4 c water
2 Tbsp butter

⎫ Combine in a saucepan. Heat until melted.

**JELLY SYRUP -**

1 c jelly
1/4 c water
3 Tbsp butter

⎫ Combine in a saucepan. Heat, stirring constantly until melted.

# All-Purpose Crêpes

1 C Baker's "Flower" ♥ ⎫
1 C milk            ⎬ Beat with a rotary
2 eggs              ⎭ beater or mix in
                      blender container.

Lightly butter a 7"-8" skillet. (Use a soft brush and melted butter).

Add about 3 Tbsp batter to the <u>heated</u> greased skillet. Tilt and rotate pan to spread batter evenly.

Bake until lightly browned - about 1 min. Flip crepe over and bake the second side for about 30 sec.

Repeat. Use a sheet of waxed paper between each crepe to stack and hold.

# Waffles

1 egg –   Break egg into a med · sized
          mixing bowl. Beat with a fork
          or whisk.

1 c milk – Add to egg, stir to blend.

2 Tbsp melted butter,          ⎫ Add. Beat with
  margarine (or vegetable oil) ⎬ whisk just till
1 ½ c Baker's "Flower" ♥       ⎭ mixed. Batter
                                 will be grainy.

Pour batter onto center of hot waffle iron
following manufacturer's directions as
to amount of batter and length of
baking time. (see QUICK BREAD TIPS)

Waffles can be baked and frozen. After
cooling, break into sections. Wrap tightly
in foil. Remove foil before heating. Place
on a baking sheet. Put into preheated
400° oven for 8-10 min.

# Thimble Doughnuts

3/4 c Baker's "Flower" ♥ ⎫
3/4 c flour          ⎬ Stir together in
1/4 c sugar          ⎪ mixing bowl. Make
1/8 tsp nutmeg       ⎭ a "well" in the center
                       of the dry mixture.

1 egg, beaten ⎫ Mix together. Pour into center
1/4 c milk    ⎭ of dry ingredients. Blend well.

Knead about 15 turns on a lightly floured
surface. The dough should stay fairly soft.

Chill for about 20 min.

Roll on a lightly floured board to a little less
than 1/4" thickness. Cut with a floured 2"
biscuit cutter. Dip thimble into flour and
cut out the center. Let set for about 20 min.

Fry in hot fat 375°. Place dried side down.
Turn as doughnuts begin to brown.
Fry 2nd side - total cooking time about 45 sec.

Drain on brown paper or cooling rack. Shake
in sugar or powdered sugar.

# Buttermilk Doughnuts

1 egg. In a mixing bowl, beat egg with a whisk or rotary beater.

1/4 c sugar
1/3 c buttermilk } Add and blend with beaten egg.

1/2 c Baker's "Flower" ♥
1/2 tsp baking soda
1/4 tsp nutmeg
1 1/4 c flour
} Blend dry ingredients before adding to the above mixture. Stir together to form dough.

Knead about 10 or 12 turns on a lightly floured board. Wrap and <u>chill</u> for 20 min.

Turn onto floured board. Flip to coat both sides. Roll or pat to 3/8" thickness.

Cut with floured doughnut cutter. Let rest, uncovered, for 20 min.

Place each cut doughnut onto a pancake turner (dried side down) and slide into deep hot fat (375°). Turn when golden brown.

Total cooking time per doughnut will be from 2-3 min.

Makes 8 large doughnuts and centers.

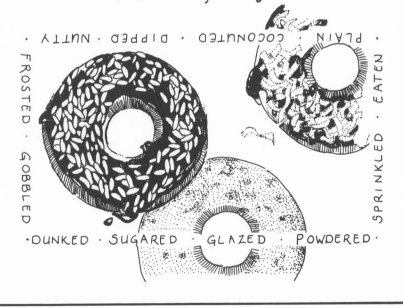

· NUTTY · DIPPED · COCONUTED · PLAIN ·
FROSTED · GOBBLED · DUNKED · SUGARED · GLAZED · POWDERED · SPRINKLED · EATEN

# Streusel Coffee Cake

350°

2 c Baker's "Flower" ♥ } Stir to blend dry ingredients
3/4 c sugar              } in a mixing bowl.

2/3 c milk - Add. Stir vigorously until light and
                  fluffy.
1 egg - Add to batter mixture. Beat until
      well-blended (about 50 strokes).
Put into a greased and floured 9" sq pan.
Sprinkle with choice of toppings below <u>before</u>
baking.
Bake 350° 30-35 min or until cake tests done
with wooden pick.

BROWN SUGAR TOPPING - 1/3 c Baker's "Flower" ♥,
  1/3 c brown sugar, packed, 1 tsp cinnamon,
  1 Tbsp butter or margarine (firm or soft) Rub
  together until crumbly.

WHITE SUGAR TOPPING - 1/2 c sugar, 1/2 c Baker's
  "Flower" ♥, 1 tsp cinnamon, 2 Tbsp butter or
  margarine. Mix dry ingredients. Rub, or
  cut in the butter.

# Banana Bread

350°

2 1/3 c Baker's "Flower" ❤
2/3 c sugar
1/4 tsp baking soda
1/4 tsp nutmeg
} Stir together in a mixing bowl.

2 eggs, beaten
2 Tbsp milk
} Add to dry ingredients. Stir till well-blended.

1 c mashed ripe bananas (2-3 med) — Add. Mix thoroughly.

(1/2 c chopped nuts)   (Add nuts) Turn into greased and floured 9x5 loaf pan.

Bake 350° 50-60 min. Bread should spring back when touched lightly in the center.

This can also be baked in 2 smaller loaf pans. Bake 40-45 min.

# Brown Bread

1 1/2 c Baker's "Flower" ❤
1 1/3 c graham wheat flour
1 tsp salt
3/4 tsp baking soda
} Stir together in a mixing bowl. Set aside.

1 egg, lightly beaten
1/3 c brown sugar, packed
1/2 c light molasses
3/4 c buttermilk
} In a separate smaller bowl, stir till well-blended. Add to dry ingredients. Mix well.

1 c chopped walnuts   — Stir walnuts into batter.

Spoon into 3 well-greased 1-lb. cans.

Bake 350° for 45 min or until bread tests done with a wooden pick. Let stand about 10 min before removing from cans to cooling rack.

This can also be baked in a 9x5 loaf pan - 50-55 min.

# Carrot Bread

350°

2½ c Baker's "Flower" ♥ ⎫ In a mixing bowl,
1 c sugar ⎬ stir to blend.
½ tsp nutmeg ⎭

2 eggs, beaten ⎫ Add to dry ingredients. Stir
¼ c milk ⎬ to make a smooth batter.

1 c chopped cooked carrots - Mix with batter.
(½ c chopped
 walnuts or pecans)    (fold in nuts)

Put in a greased and floured 9x5 loaf pan.

Bake 350° - 45 min or until bread tests done
with a wooden pick.

# Cranberry - Orange Nut Bread

3 c Baker's "flower" ♥ ⎫ Combine in a
1 c sugar ⎬ mixing bowl.

1 egg, beaten ⎫ Stir together. Add only about
1⅓ c milk ⎬ half of the liquid to the
                dry ingredients.

Using a large mixing spoon, beat about 50
vigorous strokes. Add remaining liquid in
2 parts. Stir well after each addition.

1 c fresh cranberries, halved ⎫ Add and blend
½ c chopped nuts ⎬ with the
1½ Tbsp grated orange rind ⎭ batter.

Put into a greased and floured 9x5 loaf pan.

Bake 350° - 50min - 1 hour. Bread is done
if wooden pick comes out clean.

ASSORTED NUTS

# Fruit Bread

350°

| | |
|---|---|
| 2 c finely chopped mixed dried fruits | Cover with boiling water. Soak for about 10 min. Drain well. |

| | |
|---|---|
| 2 c Baker's "Flower" ♥<br>3/4 c sugar<br>2 Tbsp butter or margarine, firm | Measure into a separate mixing bowl. Cut butter in till mixture is grainy. Toss with dried fruits. |

| | |
|---|---|
| 2 eggs, beaten<br>2 Tbsp milk<br>1/4 tsp almond extract | Add to fruit-flour mixture. Stir till thoroughly blended. |

Turn batter into a greased and floured 9 x 5 loaf pan.

Bake 350° for 50-60 min or until bread tests done with a wooden pick.

Cool 8-10 min before removing from pan.

# Irish Soda Bread

375°

1 1/3 c Baker's "Flower" ♥
1 c flour
2 Tbsp sugar
1/2 tsp baking soda
} Stir dry ingredients till blended in a mixing bowl.

1/2 c raisins - Stir raisins into dry mixture.

2/3 c buttermilk
1 egg, beaten
1/2 tsp lemon extract
} Mix together. Then, add all at once to flour mixture and stir till dough clings together.

Knead briefly on a lightly floured board. Shape into a flattened round. Place in a greased 8" round cake pan – press lightly to fit.

Cut a cross through the top to prevent cracking while baking.

Brush top with milk.

Bake 375° 30-35 min until golden brown.

# Lemon Nut Bread

350°

2 c Baker's "Flower" ♥ } Stir together in
3/4 c sugar                a mixing bowl.

1/2 c milk
2 eggs                    } Add. Beat vigorously
Finely grated rind of       with a mixing spoon
one large lemon             until smooth and fluffy.

1/3 c finely chopped pecans – stir in nuts.
Put into a greased 8 x 4 loaf pan.
<u>Bake 350°</u> 45-50 min (test with wooden pick)

<u>Glaze while hot.</u>

# Glaze

1/3 c sugar       } Stir together in a saucepan.
Juice of one        Cook and stir until sugar
 large lemon        dissolves.

Pour evenly over loaf in the pan. Cool to
room temperature. Loosen around edges.
Remove from pan to slice.

To remove "stuck" bread, set pan directly on warm
burner — just long enough to warm bottom of pan.

# Pumpkin Nut Bread

350°

1 1/2 c Baker's "Flower" ♥  ⎫
1/2 c whole wheat flour      ⎬  stir together in
1/2 tsp baking soda          ⎪  a mixing bowl.
1 tsp cinnamon               ⎪
1 c sugar                    ⎭

1/2 c milk  ⎫ Add. Stir vigorously until
2 eggs      ⎬ well-blended (50 strokes).

1 c canned pumpkin - Add to the batter.
                     Stir till thoroughly
                     mixed.

3/4 c chopped nuts - Add. Stir to mix.

Put into a greased and floured 9x5 loaf pan.

Bake 350° for 1 hour or until wooden pick
comes out clean.

Or, bake in 2 small loaf pans for about 45 min.

Yeast Breads

# About Yeast Breads

There are many variables in bread making. From the temperature in your kitchen to the temperature of your ingredients, the freshness of the yeast, the moisture content of your flour, the size of egg you add, the amount of kneading you do — all of these factors can change the way the recipes work from one time to the next.

When dissolving the yeast, the safest water temperature is <u>warmish</u>. To determine this, stick your fingertips in the water. If it feels just slightly warm to you, it's probably the correct temperature (unless, of course, you're an amphibian!) If the water is too hot, it will kill the action of the yeast.

A bit of sugar or a few drops of honey will get the yeast activated more quickly.

Stir water, yeast, and sugar until the yeast has dissolved. Let stand about 5 min.

Any ingredients which can be brought to room temperature or slightly heated will help the bread rise more quickly.

For the last addition of flour <u>before</u> kneading, mix in only enough to make the dough easy to handle.

Kneading increases the volume of the baked bread. Use as little flour as possible when kneading. Don't add more flour than the dough can absorb. The finished dough should be barely non-sticky. Too much flour makes the bread tough and dry.

While dough rests or rises, keep out of a draft or very cool area. Try to find a "warmish" spot. Cover with plastic wrap.

If using glass baking pans, reduce (preheated) oven temperature by 25 degrees. Pans should be well-greased. Remove from pans immediately after baking. Cool on racks. Cool breads thoroughly before wrapping.

# Finishing Touches for Yeast Breads

**WATER** will produce a heavy thick crust. Set a pan of warm water in the bottom of your oven while baking. Or, spray or brush with plain water (or salted water — ½ c water to 1 tsp salt) several times during the baking period. Use for French bread, breadsticks, etc.

**MILK** will give bread a nice brown color if brushed on before baking.

**BUTTER**, softened or melted, brushed on before baking or towards the end of the baking period will create a soft, brown crust.

**EGG WHITE** GLAZE can be made by mixing one unbeaten egg white with 1 Tbsp water. Brush on lightly just before baking for a crisp crust.

**EGG YOLK** GLAZE is made by beating one egg yolk with a fork and adding 1½ tsp. cold water. Stir together. Brush over breads just before baking for a shiny, golden brown crust.

**WHOLE EGG** GLAZE can be made by beating an egg with 1 tsp. water, milk, or oil. Brush on with a soft brush just before baking.

These are only some suggestions — there are many variations of these glazes.

# Recycling Baked Breads

Use an electric knife for perfectly cut thin slices of bread!

MELBA TOAST - Slice leftover homemade breads about ¼" thick. Place on ungreased baking sheet. Bake in preheated 275° oven for 15 min. Turn each slice over and bake 10 min longer. If not dry, leave bread in oven which has been <u>turned</u> <u>to</u> <u>off</u>. Close door and dry 10 min longer.

DRY BREAD CRUMBS - Bake as for Melba toast. Let cool. Then, using a rolling pin, food processor, or blender, crush into crumbs.

CROUTONS · Slice bread ½" thick. Cube. Sauté in 1-2 Tbsp butter for 2 c cubes for about 5 min. Bake in preheated 300° oven for 10 min longer. or until crisp and hard.

BREAD STUFFINGS - Slice about ½" thick. Remove crusts. Cube. Bake in 250°-275° oven until dry.

PAN·FRIED BREAD - Slice day old bread ½" thick. Spread with softened butter · Pan fry until crisp and brown (do both sides). Use as the base for an open-faced steak sandwich.

CINNAMON TOAST - Mix ¾ c sugar with 1 Tbsp cinnamon. Sprinkle over buttered toast. Put under the broiler until bubbly for a real treat!

GARLIC BREAD - Split a loaf lengthwise or cut into ¾" slices. Spread with softened or melted butter mixed with garlic juice or powder. Bake in preheated 375° oven about 8·10 min for slices.

A BREAKFAST TREAT · toast leftover slices of bread. Spread with softened cream cheese and strawberry jam.

# Shaping a Loaf of Bread

Choose pan as recipe directs. Flatten dough on a lightly floured surface into a rectangle. Make dough as wide as the pan is long. The length of the dough should be twice that measurement. For instance, if your pan is 4"x8", the dough should be rolled to 8"x 16".

← Roll from the narrow end.

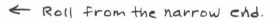

← "cut" through ends with sides of hands to seal edges.

Fold <u>pressed</u> <u>ends</u> <u>under</u>. Place seam-side down in a greased loaf pan.

← Press firmly with palm of hand to flatten and shape dough into corners.

It's ready for rising! Follow specific recipe directions.

# How to Shape Dinner Rolls

Use BASIC BREAD DOUGH. After dough has "rested", shape into rolls.

BUNS: Divide dough into 15-18 equal pieces. Shape into balls. Place on a greased sheet about 2" apart or put into greased muffin tins.

CLOVERLEAF ROLLS: Make small balls about 1" in diameter. Place 3 together in greased muffin tins.

TEA ROLLS: Form into balls about ⅓ the size you want the baked roll to be. Place close together in a greased sq or round cake pan.

When rolls are baked close together in a pan with sides, they will be soft. Set shaped rolls apart on a rimless sheet for a more crisp crust.

After shaping, brush with melted butter or margarine. Cover, let rise till slightly more than double.

Bake 375° about 20 min depending on size and shape. Remove hot rolls from pans to cooling rack.

# Basic Bread Dough

1/2 c warmish water ⎫ In a mixing bowl,
1 pkg active dry yeast ⎬ sprinkle yeast over
1/4 tsp sugar ⎭ water. Stir to dissolve.
                                Let stand about 5 min.

3/4 c milk, slightly warmed ⎫ Add to the yeast
1 egg, beaten ⎪ mixture. Beat with
1 1/2 c Baker's "Flower" ♥ ⎬ a large spoon until
3 Tbsp sugar ⎪ batter falls from it in
1 tsp salt ⎪ "sheets".
1 1/2 c flour ⎭ Or, use elec <u>mixer</u>
                                - beat 2 min on med.

(1 1/2 c flour) Add flour, 1/2 c at a time, and
                    stir vigorously after each addition.
                    Mix in enough remaining flour until
                    dough gathers. Dough will be soft.

Turn onto floured board and knead about 200 turns.

Cover with inverted mixing bowl; or, put dough into greased mixing bowl and cover with plastic wrap. Let rest 20-30 min.

Shape into DINNER ROLLS, HAMBURGER BUNS, RAISED DOUGHNUTS, CINNAMON CRISPIES, etc. See recipes which follow.

# Basic Sweet Roll Dough

Follow same directions as for BASIC BREAD DOUGH — except <u>increase sugar to 1/3 c.</u>

Shape sweet roll dough into CINNAMON ROLLS, CARAMEL PECAN ROLLS, etc.

Recipes for these and others are on the following pages.

# Easy Honey Bread Loaf

1 c warmish water  - Measure into mixing bowl.
1 pkg active dry yeast } Add. Stir till yeast
1/4 tsp sugar             has dissolved! Let
                          stand about 5 min.

2 Tbsp honey
1 c Baker's "Flower" ♥ } Add to yeast mixture.
1 c flour*                 Beat vigorously with a
1/2 tsp salt               large mixing spoon
                           about 100 strokes.

(1 c flour) · Add 1/4 c at a time and stir
well after each addition using only enough
flour to gather the dough.
Turn onto floured board. Knead about 300 turns,
using only enough flour to prevent dough from
sticking to the surface.
Turn mixing bowl over kneaded dough — let
rest 20-30 min. Shape into a loaf. Put
into a well-greased 9 X 5 loaf pan.
Brush top with softened or melted butter.
Cover with plastic wrap. Let rise until
nearly tripled.

Bake 375° (lower middle of oven) for
35-40 min.

If the top seems to be browning too
quickly, cover loosely with a piece of
aluminum foil.

If you're not certain the loaf has finished
baking, lift bread from pan — if the
bottom has a nice browned color, it's done!

Remove from pan immediately and cool
on a wire rack.

* Use any type of flour for this addition
only. Choose whole wheat, stone-ground
wheat, or just use general all-purpose flour.

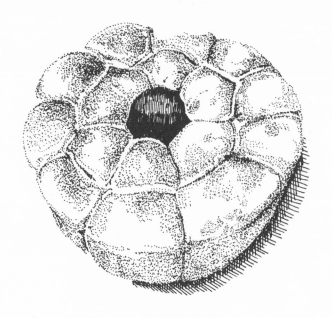

# Cheese and Garlic Bubble Loaf

Follow recipe for BASIC BREAD DOUGH.
After dough has rested, cut into 16 pieces.
Shape into balls.   Roll in cheese mixture:

> ¼ c grated parmesan cheese
> 1½ tsp dried parsley flakes
> ½ tsp garlic powder } combine
> ⅓ c butter or
>    margarine, melted

Arrange a single layer in 2 rows in a greased
tube pan <u>or</u> in two layers in a greased
9 x 5 loaf pan.

Cover loosely with plastic wrap. Let rise
till double.

After bread has risen, <u>bake at 375°</u> for
25-35 min or until golden brown.

# Hamburger Buns

Follow recipe for BASIC BREAD DOUGH.

Turn dough onto floured surface. Knead at least 3 min using as little extra flour as possible.

Cover. Let rest about 30 min.
Flatten dough on a lightly floured surface. Cut into 12 equal parts. Shape each piece into a ball.

Place on a greased jelly roll pan. Flatten to 5/8" thickness with palm of hand. If the dough springs back, press again.

Brush with melted butter or margarine. Cover loosely with plastic wrap.
Let rise until dough has nearly tripled. Bake 375° 12-15 min or until lightly browned.

Remove immediately from pan to cooling rack.

# French Doughnuts

Follow recipe for BASIC SWEET ROLL DOUGH.
Add ½ tsp nutmeg with dry ingredients.

Put finished dough into a greased bowl. Cover
and chill to firm dough.

Turn out onto floured board. Let rest for
about 10 min. Roll into a rectangle (12" x
18") about 3/8" thick. Cut into 3"x2" sections.

Cover loosely and let rise for 30 min. Dough
will not be doubled.

Heat deep fat to 375°. Fry a few at a
time until golden. brown.

Drain on brown paper. Sprinkle with sugar
or powdered sugar as desired.

# Paul Bunyon's Breakfast Rolls

Use a half recipe of BASIC BREAD DOUGH

Roll "rested" dough on a lightly floured board to about a 16" circle.
Lift carefully onto a greased 12" pizza pan.
Spoon fruit filling onto center of dough.
Lift hanging edges up and over filling leaving about a 3" opening in center.
Brush dough with milk. Sprinkle with sugar.
Do not let rise.
Bake on lowest rack of 350° oven 30-40 min. until top is golden and bottom has browned.

# Cherry Fruit Filling

1 - 16 oz can tart red cherries - Drain juice into saucepan.

2/3 c sugar } Mix till blended. Combine with
3 Tbsp cornstarch } just enough juice to make a paste. Stir back into juice in saucepan.

Cook and stir until thickened and clear.
Remove from heat; add cherries. Cool before putting on dough.

Drizzle with POWDERED SUGAR GLAZE.
3/4 c powdered sugar, 2 tsp milk, 1 tsp butter, and 1/4 tsp vanilla. Beat till smooth. Use a slotted serving spoon to drizzle over warm baked roll.

# Cinnamon Crispies

Follow recipe for BASIC BREAD DOUGH.

Roll dough on a lightly floured board to an 18"x12" rectangle.

Spread with 1 Tbsp softened butter.

Mix 1 3/4 c sugar with 1 Tbsp cinnamon. Using only 1/4 c of this mixture, sprinkle over the buttered dough.
Roll up. Cut into 12 - one inch slices.

At one side of the cutting board, sprinkle 2 Tbsp. of the remaining sugar-cinnamon mixture.

Place a sliced roll on the sugar mixture and turn to coat both sides. Using a rolling pin, roll and turn sliced dough over occasionally until very flat and about 5-6" diameter.

Set on a rimless greased cookie sheet (4-5 rolls per pan) and flatten again with rolling pin.

Cover and let rise for 30 min.

Bake 375° 15-18 min.

# Orange Slices

Follow recipe for BASIC BREAD DOUGH

Roll on a lightly floured board (after dough has rested) to an 18"x12" rectangle.
Spread with 1 Tbsp <u>softened butter</u>.

Mix ½ c sugar, ½ c finely chopped nuts, and 2 Tbsp grated orange rind. Sprinkle mixture over buttered dough.

Roll from the narrow end. Keep the roll tight. Pinch over-lapped edge to seal.
Cut into 12 - 1" slices.

At one end of the cutting board, sprinkle about 2 Tbsp sugar. Place one slice on the sugar and turn to coat both sides. Roll to a 4" diameter. Place on a foil covered baking sheet. Press with hand. <u>Do not let rise</u>.
Bake 375° 15-18 min

# Bakery Cinnamon Rolls

Follow recipe for BASIC SWEET ROLL DOUGH.

After dough has rested, roll on a lightly floured surface to 1/3" thick ( 14"x 18" rectangle).

Brush with 2 Tbsp melted butter.

Mix 1/4 c sugar with 1 1/2 tsp cinnamon and sprinkle evenly over rolled dough.

Roll up tightly beginning at <u>narrower</u> side. Push ends in to even up the ends of the roll, Cut into 12 equal pieces. Put into a greased 15x10 jelly roll pan. Press each down with palm of hand to about 1/2" thick

Cover loosely with plastic wrap. Let rise till double.

Bake 375° - middle of oven for 20-20 min.

while still warm, frost with:

2 c powdered sugar
2 Tbsp butter, softened
1/2 tsp vanilla
1/3 c milk

Measure into small mixing bowl. Add milk gradually to make a glaze-type icing.

56

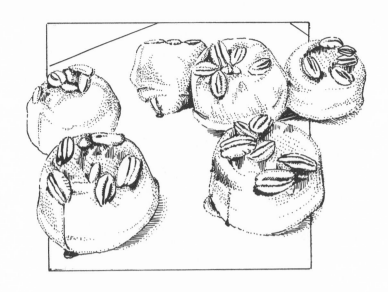

# Caramel Pecan Rolls

Follow recipe for BASIC SWEET ROLL DOUGH.

After dough has rested, roll on a lightly
floured board into a rectangle shape about
1/2" thick.
Spread 2 Tbsp softened butter or margarine
over the rolled dough.
Sprinkle with a mixture of 1/4 c sugar and
1 1/2 tsp cinnamon.
Roll tightly beginning at wide side. Cut into
15-18 slices.

Place in a greased 13x9 pan which has been
prepared with a mixture of: 1/3 c melted butter,
2/3 c brown sugar, and 2 Tbsp corn syrup.
Sprinkle 1/2 c pecan halves over the mixture.

Place sliced rolls over pecans.

Bake 375° 25-30 min. Slide knife around edges
and immediately turn upside down onto a tray.

Or, make 18 individual rolls in muffin tins. Bake
375° 15-20 min or until golden brown.

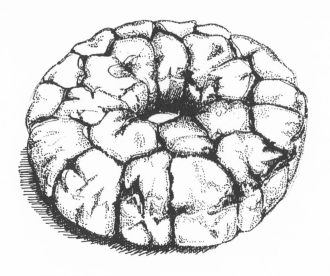

# Cinnamon Pull-Aparts

Follow recipe for BASIC SWEET ROLL DOUGH.

After dough has rested, divide into 24 pieces.

1/3 c butter or margarine, melted - Dip each piece in melted butter.

2/3 c sugar
1/3 c brown sugar, packed } Mix together. Roll dough in this mixture.
2 tsp cinnamon

Place prepared pieces in a well-greased 1-piece tube pan. Put all 24 pieces in a single layer.

Cover. Let rise until slightly more than double.

Bake 350° 30-35 min.

Let set a few min before turning out of pan.

# English Muffin Bread

3/4 c warmish water ⎫ stir to dissolve in mixing
1 pkg active dry yeast ⎬ bowl. Let stand for 5 min.
1/4 tsp sugar ⎭

1/2 c milk, slightly warmed ⎫ Add to dissolved yeast.
2/3 c Baker's "Flower" ♥ ⎬ Stir vigorously until
1 Tbsp sugar ⎪ well-mixed.
1 tsp salt ⎪
2 c flour ⎭

(1/2 c flour)  Gradually, add only enough flour
                to make dough easy to handle.
Turn onto floured board. Knead 3-5 min adding
flour as necessary.

Cover. Let rest in a warm place for about 30 min.

Shape into 1 - 9x5 loaf or 2- 7x3. Pan(s)
should be well-greased and cornmeal dusted.
Sprinkle additional cornmeal on top. Cover.
Let rise for 45 min.

To keep top from browning, cover with foil.
Cut 3 or 4 slashes to release moisture.

Bake 400° about 25 min for 9x5 loaf (20
min for smaller loaves) Remove foil. Bake 5
min longer. Remove from pan immediately. Cool
on rack.

To serve, slice and toast.

# Buttery Breadsticks

1/2 c warmish water ⎫
1/2 pkg (1 1/4 tsp) active ⎬ Stir to dissolve in
   dry yeast     ⎪ mixing bowl. Let stand
1/4 tsp sugar ⎭ till foamy - about 5 min.

1/4 c butter or ⎫
   margarine, melted ⎪ Add slightly cooled melted
1/2 c Baker's "Flower" ♥ ⎬ butter etc. to yeast
1/2 tsp salt ⎪ mixture. Stir vigorously
1 1/4 c flour ⎭ till well-blended.

(1/4 c flour for ⎫ Turn dough onto lightly floured
   kneading) ⎪ board and knead about 200 turns.
⎬ Pat into a 4"x7" rectangle. Cut
    ⎪ in half lengthwise. Then, cut
    ⎭ crosswise to make 16 sticks, 1"x2".

Roll each stick between palms of hands and
kneading surface to about 7" long.
Place on ungreased baking sheet. Let rise,
uncovered, until almost double.

<u>Bake 425°</u>(middle of oven) for 10 min. Turn oven
<u>off</u>. Leave in closed oven for 20 min. Remove.

# Dill-Cottage Cheese Bread

1/3 c warmish water⎫ Stir to dissolve
1 pkg active dry yeast⎬ in a mixing bowl.
1/4 tsp sugar⎭ Let stand 5 min.

1 egg⎫
1 c. cottage cheese,⎪
  room temperature⎪ Add to dissolved
1 Tbsp dried onion flakes⎬ yeast.
2 tsp dill seed⎪ Stir till well-blended.
2/3 c Baker's "Flower" ♥⎪
1 Tbsp sugar⎪
1/2 tsp salt⎭

1 1/2 c flour  - Add. Stir vigorously to make
             a soft dough.

(1/4- 1/2 c flour) Turn onto floured board.
              Knead about 50 turns.

Cover and let rest about 30 min.
Shape into a round or rectangle. Place
in a 1 1/2 qt buttered casserole dish or
a 9 x 5 loaf pan. Brush the top with
softened butter or margarine. Cover
and let rise until slightly more than
double.

Bake 350° 30-40 min. Remove from pan
to cooling rack.

# Whole Wheat Bread

(elec mixer)

| | |
|---|---|
| ¼ c warmish water<br>1 pkg active dry yeast<br>¼ tsp sugar | Measure into smaller bowl of elec. mixer. Stir to dissolve. Let stand for 5 min. |
| ¾ c milk, slightly warmed<br>2 Tbsp honey<br>½ tsp salt<br>½ c Baker's "Flower" ❤<br>1 c whole wheat flour<br>(or stone-ground) | Add to dissolved yeast. Blend on low speed scraping bottom and sides of bowl. Beat 2 min. on high speed. |

( ¾ c flour) - Stir in only enough flour to make a soft dough.

Put some of the remaining flour on a kneading surface. Turn dough onto flour. Knead about 50 turns adding flour as necessary to prevent sticking.

Place in a greased 8x4 loaf pan, or shape into buns and bake in a 9" sq pan.

Brush tops with butter. Cover. Let rise till doubled - 1-2 hours.

<u>Bake</u> 375° ~ Bread loaf - 35 min. Rolls - 20-25 min.

DELI SANDWICH • DELI SANDWICH •
• CORNED BEEF • HAM & SWISS •
DELI SANDWICH
TOMATO LETTUCE
RUEBEN • PASTRAMI • DELI SANDWICH
• SALAMI • KOSHER PICKLE •
DELI SANDWICH • DELI SANDWICH

# Light Rye Bread

| | |
|---|---|
| 1 c warmish water<br>1 pkg active dry yeast<br>¼ tsp sugar | stir to dissolve in a mixing bowl. Let stand for about 5 min. |
| 1 tsp caraway seed<br>1 Tbsp brown sugar<br>1 tsp salt<br>⅓ c Baker's "Flower" ♥<br>1 c flour<br>1 c light rye flour | Add to dissolved yeast mixture. Stir till well blended. |
| (¼ c flour) | Sprinkle some flour on kneading surface. Knead 3-5 min adding more flour as necessary. |

Cover. Let rest about 30 min.
Shape into a flattened round. Place in a grease 8" pie pan. Grease top of loaf. Slash 3 times about ⅛" deep using a sharp knife or razor blade.

Cover loosely with plastic wrap. Let rise till slightly more than double.

Bake 350° 35-45 min. Remove from pan. Cool on rack.

# Sourdough Bread

I've collected several recipes for sourdough starters. I selected this particular one because it says it does not have to be refrigerated. You don't have to plan ahead to use it; therefore, it will probably be used more often. For those of you unfamiliar with sourdough baking, the bread is made in stages. The first is ongoing.

Here is the recipe for the first stage — this is called the <u>starter</u>.

2 c warmish water } In a mixing bowl,
1 pkg active dry yeast } sprinkle yeast over
1 tsp sugar } the water. Add sugar. Stir to dissolve.

2 c flour (all-purpose — Stir in. Beat until
or bread flour) smooth.

Put into a wide-mouthed glass or earthenware container. Cover loosely. Set in a warm place (such as a countertop near your oven and/or range) for <u>at least 3 days</u> before using.

If the mixture separates, stir it down. Always leave at least one cup of starter in the container. If you have not used it for one week, remove <u>all but one</u> cup from the container and discard the extra part. Add 1 c flour and 1 c warmish water to the remaining one cup starter and blend well.

Over a period of time, the starter may lose some of its rising power. If this happens, dissolve 1 tsp yeast in ¼ c water. Add to the container and stir well. If that doesn't reactivate it, throw it away and make a new batch.

Remember, each time you take from it you must add back to it in equal portions of flour and water - ¾ to 1 c of each.

After your starter has "soured" for at least 3 days, you will be ready for stage 2 — this part is called the sponge.

| | |
|---|---|
| 1 c Sourdough starter<br>2 1/2 c flour<br>2 c warm water | Combine in a large glass or earthenware bowl and beat with a mixing spoon to make a smooth batter |

Cover with plastic wrap and let stand in a warm place for 8 hours. Depending on your schedule, it can be started either at night or in the morning. Then finish it eight hours later — whichever is most convenient for you.

3rd stage - Eight (or thereabouts) hours later:

To the sponge, add:

| | |
|---|---|
| 1 c Baker's "Flower" ♥<br>2 Tbsp sugar<br>3/4 tsp salt<br>2 1/2 c flour | Stir together until the dough begins to mass. |

Put onto a floured board. Knead for about 10 min adding flour as necessary to keep dough from sticking. Put dough into a large greased bowl. Turn dough to bring greased side up.

Cover with plastic wrap. Let rise in a warm place until double.

Punch down and divide into halves. Shape each into a round loaf. Place both on a large greased baking sheet on opposite corners. With a sharp knife or razor blade cut three 1/8" slashes across top of each loaf.

Let rise, uncovered, until double (45 min - 1 hour) Brush or spray loaves with cold water.

Bake 375° for 50 min in center of oven — check to see if bottom has browned. Remove from pan to cooling rack.

Makes 2 loaves

# Easy Danish Pastry

½ c warmish water
1 pkg active dry yeast
¼ tsp sugar
} stir to dissolve in a mixing bowl. Let stand for about 5 min.

½ c evaporated milk
¼ c sugar
2 eggs, beaten
} Stir into yeast mixture. Chill.

1¼ c Baker's "Flower" ♥
2½ c flour
} In a separate mixing bowl, blend flours.

¾ c butter - Cut into dry ingredients with a pastry blender to form small pebbles.

Combine with chilled mixture. Cover and refrigerate about 20 min.
Roll on a lightly floured board ⅛-¼" thick.
Cut into ½" strips. Twist lengthwise. Form into pinwheels, pretzels, or other shapes.
Fill centers with 1 Tbsp preserves. (Shape on a greased baking sheet)
Let rise for 45 min - uncovered.
Bake 400° 10-12 min. Remove pastries to a cooling rack.

Drizzle with powdered sugar icing, if desired.
(Mix 1 c powdered sugar with 1½-2 Tbsp milk)

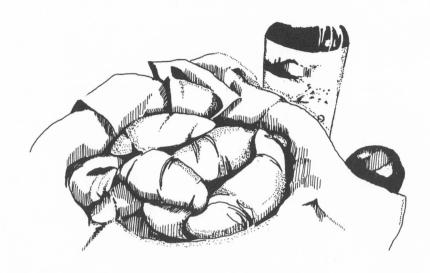

# Crescent Rolls

Make dough as for EASY DANISH PASTRY.
Divide in half. Roll out on a lightly floured
board to a ¼" thick square.

Cut into triangle shapes as diagrammed below.
(Or, roll into a circle and cut in 8 wedges)

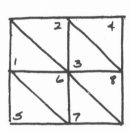

Roll from wide end. Place on
a greased baking sheet. Curve
to form a crescent shape.

Brush with melted butter or an egg wash. (Make
egg wash by beating 1 egg yolk with 1½ Tbsp milk).
Let rise for 45 min.

Bake 375° 12-15 min until golden brown.

The following breads have been grouped together at the end of the yeast breads because they are used in some of the MAIN DISH recipes in the next section.

It is hoped that it will be easier for you to remember where they are and, therefore, easier for you to locate them.

They include; a RUSTIC BREAD LOAF which can also be found in the MAIN DISH section under the name HAM AND CHEESE BREAD LOAF. There is a basic recipe from which CRACKER-BREAD, TRADITIONAL BREADSTICKS, AND PITA BREAD can all be made. You'll find SOPAIPILLAS - puffy deep-fried little pillows. These can be filled with HONEY-BUTTER and served as a sweet pastry or stuffed with meats and cheeses.

You'll also find PIZZA CRUSTS in this section. One is for a regular crust pizza and is called EASY-MIX PIZZA CRUST. CALZONE (in the MAIN DISH SECTION) is made from this dough. There's a DEEP-DISH PIZZA CRUST and a CORNMEAL PIZZA CRUST. Toppings can be found in MAIN DISHES. The CORNMEAL CRUST is used as a base for a Mexican pizza or rolled around hot dogs and baked.

# Rustic Bread Loaf

1 c warmish water
1 pkg active dry yeast
¼ tsp sugar
} Stir to dissolve in a mixing bowl. Let stand for 5 min.

½ c Baker's "Flower" ♥
1 tsp salt
2 c flour
} Add to the dissolved yeast mixture. Stir till well-mixed.

(additional flour for mixing and kneading)  — Use enough extra flour to gather the dough.

Lightly flour a kneading surface. Turn dough onto it. Knead for about 3 min.

Cover. Let rest for 30 min. or thereabouts.

Shape like a french or Vienna type bread, or, as desired. Use a sharp knife or razor blade to cut ⅛" deep slashes.

Let rise, uncovered, until slightly more than double.   Bake 375° 30-35 min.

69

# Cracker Bread

3/4 c warmish water
1/2 pkg (1¼ tsp) active
  dry yeast
¼ tsp sugar
}
Stir to dissolve in a
mixing bowl. Let stand
for about 5 min.

2 Tbsp vegetable oil
½ c Baker's "Flower" ♥
1 tsp salt
}
Add to dissolved yeast.
Stir together.

1½ c flour    – Add. Stir vigorously
(½ c flour)    If necessary, add more flour to
               form a soft dough – enough to
               make dough gather together.

Sprinkle the remainder of the flour — using extra
if necessary, onto the kneading surface.
Turn dough onto floured surface and knead about
200 turns.

Cover. Let rest about 30 min. Divide into 4 balls.
Roll one at a time (keep remaining dough covered)
onto a <u>rimless</u> greased sheet to a <u>very thin</u> 10-12"
diameter. Prick well.

Bake immediately on lower middle rack of a
425° oven for 7-10 min, until golden brown.

After cooling, return to a 275° oven and dry about
10 min longer or until crisp. (if needed).

# Traditional Breadsticks

Follow recipe for CRACKER BREAD. dough.

After kneading, pat into a 4"x7" rectangle on a floured surface. Cut in half lengthwise. Then, cut crosswise to make 16 sticks.

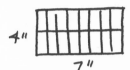

4"

7"

Take one of the "sticks" and roll between kneading surface and palm of hand to about a 7" length.

Place on greased baking sheet. Repeat with remaining sticks. Leave space for rising and baking.

Brush with an egg white glaze or with water before baking if desired.

Let rise, uncovered, until <u>almost</u> <u>double</u>.

Bake 425° for 12-15 min. For an extra-crisp breadstick, turn <u>off</u> the oven <u>after</u> <u>baking</u> and leave in 5-10 min longer.

# Pita Bread

Follow recipe for CRACKER BREAD dough.

After dough has rested, divide into 8 equal parts. Shape into balls. Dusting lightly with flour, as necessary, roll each to a 5"-6" diameter.

Place on a flat baking sheet which has been sprinkled with cornmeal. (Leave enough space between each so they will not touch when baking).

Cover loosely with plastic wrap. Let rise 30 min.

Bake 450° middle or lower middle of oven for 5-10 min or until puffed and lightly browned.

# Sopaipillas

¼ c warmish water
1 pkg active dry yeast } Stir to dissolve in a mixing bowl. Let stand for 5 min.
¼ tsp sugar

1¼ c milk,
  slightly warmed
2/3 c Baker's "Flower" ♥ } Add to yeast mixture. Stir just till mixed.
3 ½ c flour

Turn dough onto floured surface. Knead 15-20 turns.

Cover with plastic wrap or invert bowl over dough. Let rest for 10 min.

Heat  3-4  c vegetable oil to about 400°

Roll ¼ of the dough ¼" thick. Cut into 12 squares with a pizza cutter. Stretch each piece slightly and place rolled side down into hot oil. Fry till golden brown. Drain on rack or brown paper. Repeat.

(These can be prepared ahead and frozen)

If you have frozen the SOPAIPILLAS, place desired amount on a baking pan. Reheat in a preheated 375° oven for 5-8 min. or until crisp and hot.

## SERVING OPTIONS:

When SOPAIPILLAS are still warm from frying, shake them in a sugar-cinnamon mixture. Serve as a breakfast bread or as a dessert.

They can also be used as an appetizer or main dish when stuffed with cheese fillings or refried beans.

Or, they are especially delicious when served with the following HONEY-BUTTER!

# Honey-Butter

½ c butter
(let it set at
room temperature
for 20-25 min)

Using the smaller bowl of your electric mixer, cream slightly firm butter until it begins to get fluffy.

⅓ c honey

G·r·a·d·u·a·l·l·y add honey and continue beating until light and fluffy.

Serve chilled or at room temperature with hot SOPAIPILLAS.

# Tips on Pizza Making

As with all yeast breads — <u>don't</u> <u>add</u> <u>too</u> <u>much</u> <u>flour</u> — you'll get a crust that is tough and dry.

Unless your flour is extremely dry, the 1⅓c in the EASY-MIX PIZZA crust should work in easily.

There are some options when making the crust. You can do the minimum kneading right in the bowl (if your mixing bowl is not too deep or too narrow). If you're in a rush, go ahead without letting the dough rest and press immediately into the greased pan. (Use extra flour, if necessary, when shaping). Form a ridge around the edge. Top and bake.

Or, if you can spare the time, knead it for 2-3 min — then, cover, and let it rest for 5-10 min. <u>Roll</u> on a floured surface just a little larger than the pan's diameter. Put into pan, shape, and form a ridge around edge.

For a crisp, brown bottom on your crust, it is absolutely essential that you use a heavy-weight, preferably dark colored, pizza pan. (You might prefer a pizza stone). Be sure to grease the pan (not the stone). You can sprinkle with cornmeal, if you'd like.

The toppings are really a matter of personal taste. In the MAIN DISH SECTION, you will find 2 BASIC PIZZA SAUCE recipes — one for deep dish and one for regular crust.

# Easy-Mix Pizza Crust

2/3 c warmish water
1/2 pkg (1¼ tsp) active
  dry yeast
¼ tsp sugar
} Stir to dissolve in a mixing bowl. Let stand for about 5 min.

1 Tbsp butter or
  margarine, softened
⅓ c Baker's "Flower" ♥
½ tsp salt
1⅓ c flour
} Add to yeast mixture. Stir vigorously until dough clings together.

Turn onto a lightly floured board. Knead a minimum of 20·30 turns. Cover with plastic wrap or inverted bowl. Let rest 5·10 min.

Roll (or pat) to fit a well-greased 14" pizza pan – see TIPS ON PIZZA MAKING. (Or, shape 2-4 smaller pizzas).

Variation: WHOLE-WHEAT CRUST
  Use 2/3 c whole wheat flour plus 2/3 c all-purpose flour (instead of the total 1⅓ c flour).

# Deep-Dish Pizza Crust

1 c warmish water
1/2 pkg (1 1/4 tsp) active dry yeast
1/2 tsp sugar

} Stir to dissolve in a mixing bowl. Let stand about 5 min.

2 Tbsp butter or margarine, very soft
1/3 c Baker's "Flower" ♥
3/4 tsp salt
2 c flour

} Add to dissolved yeast. Stir vigorously with a large spoon.

Knead on a floured surface from 3-4 min.

Put into a greased bowl and cover with plastic wrap. Let rest 25-30 min.

Pat onto a greased 12" deep dish pizza pan

How to top, See MAIN DISH section

# Cornmeal Pizza Crust

1/2 pkg (1 1/4 tsp) active dry yeast
2/3 c warmish water
1/2 tsp sugar

} Measure water into mixing bowl. Sprinkle with yeast and sugar. Stir to dissolve. Let stand 5 min.

1 Tbsp butter or margarine, very soft
1 tsp salt
1/2 c Baker's "Flower" ♥
1/4 c cornmeal
1 c flour

} Add. Beat vigorously until dough forms.

Knead on a lightly floured board.

Press onto a greased 14-16" pizza pan, or roll and shape to fit.

Use with traditional pizza toppings or refer to MAIN DISH section for a Mexican-type pizza or hot dog "buns".

# Main & Side Dishes

## Appetizers
## Sauces
## Soups

ORE REGAN ANO OR AGANO

# PIZZA TOPPINGS

Remember to shape the dough in a heavy dark pizza pan or on a pizza stone for the most crispy brown crust.

If you don't have a great pizza pan, you might want to partially bake the crust before topping. After shaping, prick well with a fork and bake the crust at 475° on the lowest oven rack for 8 or 9 min. Put sauce and other toppings on and return it to a 475° oven for 12-15 min longer or until cheese is hot and bubbly.

Otherwise, spoon sauce over the shaped but unbaked crust — use about 1 c for a 14" pizza

Sprinkle extra seasonings on, if desired — such as oregano or basil or black pepper.

The mozzarella cheese comes next — use about 8 oz (sliced or shredded) and put evenly over the sauce. (2 c shredded)

Extra optional toppings:
  Green and/or red peppers, thinly sliced
  Spanish onion, thinly sliced
  pepperoni, thinly sliced
      and/or sweet Italian sausage, browned & drained
      and/or hamburger, browned and drained
  fresh mushrooms, cleaned and sliced
  ripe or green olives
  anchovy fillets, well-drained
  More mozzarella (about 4oz) or a sprinkling
      of parmesan cheese.
(Drizzle a bit of olive oil over the top)

Bake 475° lowest oven rack about 20 min for unbaked Easy-Mix Pizza Crust.

# Traditional Pizza Sauce

1 - 6oz can tomato paste ~ Put into a 2c
                                       glass measure.

Water  -   Add water, a bit at a time, blending
                   well between additions until the
                   combined mixture measures 2c.

1 tsp dried crushed basil leaves
½ tsp dried crushed oregano   } Add to diluted paste.
1 tsp onion powder
⅛ tsp garlic powder   } stir to blend.
(a few crushed fennel seeds)

Put all ingredients in a saucepan, bring to a boil,
stirring often. Reduce heat to low and simmer
about 20 min, stirring occasionally.

<u>Cool</u> to room temperature before using.

                         2 c sauce

# "Sauce" for Deep-Dish Pizza

1- 16 oz can of quartered        - Drain well. Remove
   tomatoes (or Italian plum tomatoes)  seeds, if
                                        desired.(Chop,
                                        if necessary)

Spread quartered (or chopped) tomatoes evenly
over prepared DEEP-DISH PIZZA dough.

¼ c grated parmesan cheese ⎫ sprinkle over
2 tsp basil leaves, crushed ⎬ the tomatoes.
1 tsp oregano leaves, crushed ⎭

Top with:

1½ c shredded mozzarella cheese
and any other desired toppings such as
thinly sliced onions, pepperoni, mushrooms,
green pepper, ripe olives, etc.

Sprinkle with more mozzarella cheese (1-1½c)

Bake 425°  25 min until crust has browned.

Cut into wedges for serving.

# Calzone

Follow recipe for EASY-MIX PIZZA CRUST.
Knead as for rolled pizza dough.
Cover and let rest while preparing filling.
(or prepare filling <u>before</u> making the
dough, and you can rest, too!

Filling:

    ½ c ricotta cheese - whip till fluffy
    1 egg, beaten - reserve 1 Tbsp to glaze
                  the calzone. Mix remainder
                  with the ricotta cheese.
    2 Tbsp chopped fresh parsley
    2 Tbsp chopped green onion    ) Stir in
    ½ lb shredded mozarella cheese } with ricotta-
    ¼ c grated parmesan cheese   / egg mixture.
    3-4 oz chopped pepperoni.

Divide dough in half. Shape each into
flattened rounds and roll on a lightly
floured board to a 12" diameter. Lift
and add flour as needed to keep dough
from sticking.

Place on a greased jelly roll pan.
Put half of the filling on one side of
the pastry — like a turnover — leave space to crimp.
Mix the reserved 1 Tbsp egg with 1 tsp water.
Brush around the edge. Fold dough and
press with tines of fork to seal.
Make 3 slashes about 1" long on top of each.
Brush with egg mixture.

<u>Bake</u> 400° for 25 min or until golden brown.

Makes 2 large turnovers.

There are many different fillings for Calzone —
this is only one suggestion.

# Ole' ⚘ Ole' ⚘ Ole'

## Taco Pizza

Make CORNMEAL PIZZA CRUST dough - see
YEAST BREADS

Knead dough using only enough flour to
keep dough from sticking.

Cover and let rest for 15-20 min.

In the meantime, prepare the topping.

> ½ lb sausage or - Brown crumbled meat.
>    hamburger        Drain well.

> 1 c refried beans - Combine beans with
>                       the browned meat.

> 2½ c grated cheese - Grate Set aside.
>    Mozzarella, Cheddar
>    and/or Monterrey Jack

Roll pizza dough onto a floured board to a
14"-16" diameter (or make smaller pizzas for
individual servings). Place on greased pan. Prick.

Bake crust only 425° for 10 min

Top partially baked crust with sausage-bean
mixture. Sprinkle cheese over that.

Return to 425° oven. Bake 10-20 min
longer until cheese has melted and
crust is brown.

Top baked taco pizza with:

>          Shredded lettuce
>          chopped tomatoes
>          Grated cheddar cheese
>          Com chips
>          Taco Sauce

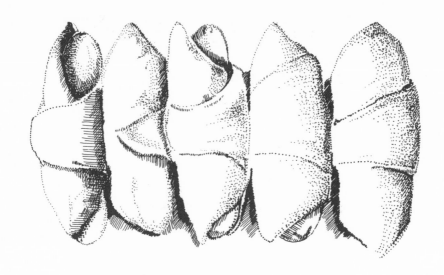

# "Red Hot" Line-up

Make CORNMEAL PIZZA CRUST dough - see YEAST BREADS

Divide dough into 2 equal parts. Shape into flattened rounds. Roll each on a lightly floured board to a 9"-10" diameter. Cut each into 4 or 5 wedges depending on number of hot dogs (8-10).

Place a hot dog across the wide end of the triangle and roll up in the dough.

Place lapped side down on a lightly greased baking sheet about ½" apart.

Brush with melted butter. Cover loosely with plastic wrap. Let rise in a warm place for about 20 min. Uncover.

Bake 400° - 20 min or until golden brown.

Serve with dipping condiments.

# Ham and Cheese Bread Loaf

Make RUSTIC BREAD LOAF dough - see YEAST BREAD section.

Cover. Let dough rest for about 30 min. Prepare Filling.

FILLING:

3/4 c ground or finely chopped ham
2 c grated swiss cheese (8oz)
1 egg, beaten (reserve ½ tbsp for glaze)
⅛ tsp onion powder
dash of nutmeg
} Combine in a bowl. Set aside

Roll dough on a lightly floured surface to an 8" x 14" rectangle.

Put filling on center - leaving about 1½" above and below. Fold those edges over filling.

Bring sides together and overlap about 1". Seal edge. Turn seam-side down onto greased jelly roll pan.

Cut slashes through the top. Brush with reserved egg mixed with 1 tsp water. Do not let rise.

Bake 375° 30-35 min or until golden brown.

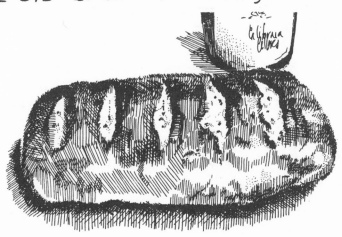

# Flour Tortillas

1 1/2 c flour
2/3 c Baker's "Flower" ♥ } Stir together in a mixing bowl.

2/3 c cold water · Add water all at once. Stir rapidly to form a stiff dough.

Knead a few turns to work in any remaining flour. Shape into a ball.

Flatten slightly on a lightly floured board. Cut into 8 equal triangles. Shape into 8 balls. Cover with plastic wrap and let rest about 10 min.

Roll each out on a lightly floured board until very thin (8" diameter). Turn and flour as needed to prevent dough from sticking to rolling surface.

Bake on ungreased griddle over med. heat about 1 1/2-2 min per side. They will have small brown spots when baked.

See recipes following for ways to serve.

# Main Dish Taco Salad

Make FLOUR TORTILLA dough. After rolling, cut into quarters with a pizza cutter. (Do not griddle-bake). Drop a few at a time, do not crowd, into 1" hot vegetable oil (375°). Fry until puffy and golden.

Prepare fried tortillas ahead. Reheat in oven.

1 lb ground round beef (desired seasonings) — Brown. Drain grease. Keep warm.

2-3 tomatoes, chopped
1/2 c diced onion
1/4 c ripe olives, sliced
1 ripe avocado, chopped
1 head lettuce, shredded

Toss vegetables with hamburger just before serving.

Put into 4 large salad bowls.

Grated cheddar cheese
Taco sauce

- Top each with cheese and sauce.

Serve with hot, crisp flour tortillas.

# Oven 'Fried' Chimichangas

Prepare griddle-baked FLOUR TORTILLAS.

Leftover beef or pork roast
Gravy, salsa sauce, or taco sauce
Refried beans
(Sauteed onions)

Combine whatever you choose to make a filling. Allow 1/2 c per large tortilla.

Melted butter or margarine — 1 Tbsp per each large tortilla. Brush both sides with the melted butter.

Divide filling among the tortillas. Spoon 1/2 c onto center of each. Fold ends up and over, then over-lap sides. Place seam-side down in a baking pan.

Bake 500° 8-10 min or until golden. Sprinkle with grated cheddar cheese. Serve with sour cream, guacamole etc.

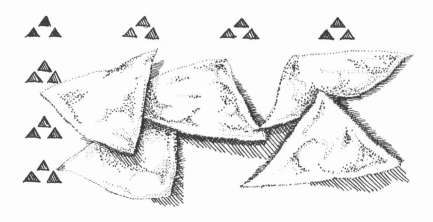

# Tortilla 'Snacks'

<u>PARMESAN TORTILLAS</u> - Make FLOUR TORTILLAS. Bake on griddle. (This can be done ahead).

Quarter or cut into strips. Brush with melted butter. Sprinkle with onion powder and parmesan cheese. Place on baking sheet.

<u>Bake 250°</u> 20-30 min or until dry and crisp

<u>"SOUTH-OF-THE-BORDER" APPETIZER</u> - Cut griddle baked FLOUR TORTILLAS into quarters. Brush with hot taco sauce, sprinkle with grated Monterrey Jack cheese.

Put on a lightly greased baking sheet.

<u>Bake 375°</u> 6-8 min or until edges begin to brown.

<u>CINNAMON CRISPS</u> - After rolling flour tortillas, cut into quarters with a pizza cutter. (<u>Do not</u> griddle bake.) Fry in 1" <u>hot</u> 375° vegetable oil. Do not crowd. Fry until puffy and golden, Drain on brown paper. Shake in a mixture of 3/4 c sugar and 1 Tbsp cinnamon.

# Easy Dumplings

1 1/2 c Baker's "Flower" ♥  - Measure into
                                    mixing bowl.

1/2 c milk - Add milk all at once. Stir
                until well-blended.
Drop by spoonfuls onto gently bubbling stews.

Cook, uncovered, for 10 min. Reduce heat. Cover
and simmer gently for 10 min longer.
                         8-10 dumplings

# Egg Dumplings

1 1/3 c Baker's "Flower" ♥  - Measure into
                                    mixing bowl.
1 egg, beaten ⎫ Combine. Add all at once. Stir
1/4 c milk    ⎭ until well-blended.

Drop by rounded tablespoonfuls onto gently
boiling stews.

Cook, uncovered, for 10 min. Reduce heat. Cover
and simmer gently for 10 min longer.
                         8-10 dumplings

. . . . . . .

Dip spoon into broth before dipping into
dumpling batter - it will slide off more easily.

Drop onto meat or vegetables — not directly
into liquid.

SOUP  DU  JOUR  •  SOUP  DU  JOUR  •  SOUP

# Homemade Pasta

2 c flour  
1/2 c Baker's "Flower" ♥  } stir together in a mixing bowl.

3 eggs, beaten  
1/4 c water  } Combine. Add all at one time to flour mixture. Stir till well-blended. Use hands if difficult to mix.

Turn onto floured board. Knead in enough additional flour to make a stiff dough. Cover. Let rest about 20 min.

Divide into 3 parts. Roll thin as possible on a floured board. Turn dough over while rolling and add extra flour as needed to prevent sticking. Repeat.

Let each "sheet" dry from 30 min-4 hours on a towel covered oven rack (remove from oven to counter or table top). Turn once.

Fold over jelly roll style (you may need to sprinkle lightly with flour) to form a flat roll. about 3" wide. Cut into strips 1/8"-1/3" wide. Unroll strips and spread out on towel covered rack.

To cook: Bring 3 qts water with 1/2 Tbsp salt to a rapid boil. Add half of the noodles. Return to a boil and cook, uncovered, 3-10 min. Cooking time will depend on size and dryness of noodles. Stir occasionally to prevent sticking. Drain well in colander. Do not rinse. Serve immediately with desired sauce.

To freeze: Spread cut noodles on a cookie sheet and put in freezer. When frozen, put into a plastic bag, close tightly and return to freezer.

# Pesto Sauce for Homemade Pasta

1/4 c butter or
  margarine, softened
1/4 c grated parmesan cheese
1/2 c finely chopped parsley
1 clove garlic, crushed
1 tsp dried crushed basil leaves

} Measure into mixing bowl. Use a spoon to blend ingredients.

1/4 c olive or vegetable oil - Add oil to the above mixture while stirring constantly.

1/4 c chopped walnuts - Mix in nuts.

Add to <u>hot</u> noodles and toss till well-coated. (Enough sauce for a half recipe - 8 oz - cooked, drained Homemade Pasta).

# Creamy Italian Sauce

1/2 lb bacon - Cut into small pieces. Sauté while noodles cook. Drain all but 2 Tbsp grease. Remove from heat.

1 recipe HOMEMADE PASTA - Cook and drain as (or 10-12 oz. store-bought) recipe directs.

Add to bacon in skillet - turn heat to low. Toss with freshly ground pepper, salt, and finely chopped garlic to your taste.

2 eggs
1 1/2 c cream

} Beat together. Stir into <u>hot</u> noodles.

1/2 c grated parmesan cheese - Stir in cheese. Remove from heat. Serve hot.

# Pasta Salad

Mix 8 oz. cooked, well-drained pasta with 1 1/2 - 2 c desired crisp-cooked vegetables (broccoli flowerettes, peas, carrots) and 1/4 c each sliced black olives and parmesan cheese.

Combine 1/2 c of your favorite garlic dressing with 1/2 c mayonnaise and toss gently with pasta. Refrigerate. Add fresh tomatoes just before serving.

# Noodle Dumplings

1 c Baker's "Flower" ♥ } stir together in a
2/3 c flour            mixing bowl.

1 egg, beaten - Beat egg in a glass measuring cup.
Milk  -  Add milk to equal ½ c. Add to dry
          ingredients. Mix well. Knead briefly.

Roll out on a well-floured board to no more
than ¼" thickness. (Turn over and add flour
as needed to prevent sticking).

Cut with pastry cutter or pizza cutter into
desired size.

Drop by handfuls into gently boiling stews,
soups, or soup stock. Cook until done - from
5-10 min depending on size.

These can be cooked immediately after rolling,
or they can stand for awhile if tossed
gently with extra flour and loosely scattered.

# Quick Quiche Lorraine

4 eggs, beaten
1¼ c milk          } Beat together with whisk
½ tsp salt         } or rotary beater.
⅛ tsp nutmeg

1 c diced cooked ham     } Add to the egg
  (or ½ lb. crisp fried  } mixture. Stir to
  crumbled bacon)        } blend.
2 Tbsp chopped green onion

1¼ c shredded swiss cheese  } Shake together to
¼ c Baker's "Flower" ♥      } coat cheese. Mix
                              with other ingredients

Put into a buttered quiche pan, 10" pie pan, or
9" sq pan.

<u>Bake</u> <u>375°</u> for 45 min. Let set 5 min before
serving. (Reduce heat to 350° for glass pans)


# Italian Quiche

Substitute cooked well-drained sweet sausage
or ¼ c chopped pepperoni for the ham. Omit
nutmeg, add ½ tsp crushed dried basil leaves.
Add ½ c fresh chopped tomato. Substitute
mozzarella cheese. Follow above directions.


# Mexican Quiche

Substitute ¼ c finely chopped pepperoni for
the ham. Omit nutmeg, add 1 tsp chili
powder. Add ½ c chopped fresh tomato.
Substitute Monterrey Jack and/or cheddar
cheese for the swiss. Follow above directions.

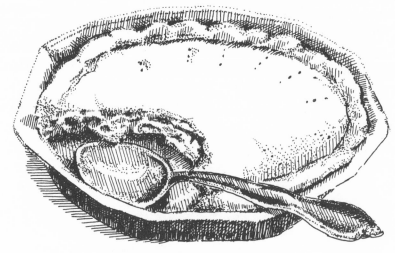

# Pot Pie Pastry

1 1/4 c flour ⎫ Blend dry ingredients
1/4 c Baker's "Flower" ♥ ⎬ in a mixing bowl.
1/4 tsp salt ⎭

1/3 c vegetable oil ⎫ Combine egg and
2 Tbsp beaten egg ⎬ oil in a glass
  (reserve remainder) ⎭ measuring cup.
Milk   - <u>Add</u> milk to equal 2/3 c. Stir
        liquids together.

Add all at once to the dry ingredients. Mix with a fork until dough cleans sides of bowl. Shape into a ball.

Roll between 2 sheets of waxed paper to desired size and shape. (This will make enough pastry for a 10" pie plate or four individual tart size pies).

Remove top paper. Invert over filling and gently lift off the second piece of paper.

Trim and shape edge. Prick top or cut slashes to vent steam.

Brush with remaining egg mixed with 1 tsp water.

Bake large pie 350 degrees for about 45 min or until the crust is golden brown.

# Pot Pie Filling

1 ½ - 2 c <u>cooked</u> meat
  cut into chunky pieces
  (turkey, chicken, or
  leftover roast beef)
1 ½ - 2 c cooked vegetables
  (peas, carrots, corn, etc)
1 ½ - 2 c leftover gravy
  (or 1 can cream of chicken,
  celery or mushroom soup)
¼ c stock or milk
Seasoning to taste

Combine all ingredients.

Put into a buttered 9" sq. baking dish. Top with pastry.

Bake 350° for about 45 min or until crust is golden brown.

<u>Variation</u>: Add ¼ c diced onion and 2-4 Tbsp diced green pepper which have been sautéed in a couple Tbsp of butter or margarine with above ingredients.

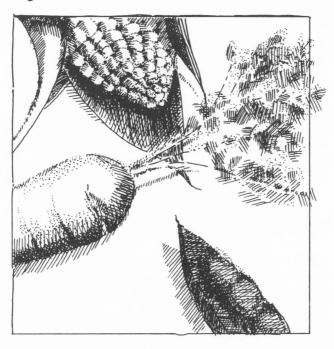

# Seasoned Coating for Pan-Fried Meats

| | |
|---|---|
| ½ c Baker's "Flower" ♥<br>½ c flour<br>1 ½ tsp salt<br>¼ tsp pepper | Combine in a plastic or paper bag. Shake to thoroughly mix. |

Roll or shake pork chops, chicken pieces, round steak etc in the mixture.

Set on waxed paper while shortening heats.

| | |
|---|---|
| Vegetable oil<br>(3-4 Tbsp)<br>Butter or margarine<br>(3-4 Tbsp) | You'll need at least ¼" melted shortening. The exact amount will depend on the size of your skillet. Stir, or tilt pan, to blend. |

Place flour coated meat in <u>hot</u> grease.

Cover skillet <u>loosely</u> while frying to speed cooking and reduce splattering.

Fry until crisp, brown, and tender. Choice of meat will determine cooking time.

# Pan-Fried Fish

1 1/2 - 2 lbs fish fillets

3/4 c flour
1/4 c Baker's "Flower" ♥ ⎫ shake dry ingredients
1 tsp salt ⎬ in a plastic or
1/4 tsp pepper ⎭ brown paper bag.

1 egg, beaten ⎫ Mix together. Pour into a
1 Tbsp water ⎭ shallow container.

Dip fish (both sides) into egg mixture. Then, coat with flour mixture. (cut sides of bag and open flat to expose dry ingredients).

Set prepared fish fillets on a flat baking sheet (or on waxed paper) while grease heats.

Heat equal portions of vegetable oil and butter or margarine in a skillet. Tilt to blend as it melts - should be about 1/8" deep.

Place fish in hot grease over med-high heat. Cook until brown and crisp - about 6 min. Turn carefully, brown other side. Total frying time will be about 10 min.

Variation - Substitute 3/4 c yellow cornmeal for the flour.

# Seasoned Salt

1/2 c salt
1 Tbsp garlic salt ⎫ Shake or blend
1 Tbsp paprika ⎪ together.
1 Tbsp sugar ⎬
1 tsp white pepper ⎪ Store in a small
1 tsp cornstarch ⎪ tightly closed
1/4 tsp tumeric ⎭ container.

Use with OVEN-FRIED CHICKEN flour mix or in any recipe calling for seasoned salt. Great for cereal snack party mix!

# Oven-Fried Chicken

425°

| | |
|---|---|
| ½ c Baker's "Flower" ♥<br>½ c flour<br>1 Tbsp seasoned salt<br>⅛ tsp pepper | Combine dry ingredients in a plastic or brown bag. Shake till blended. |
| whole fryer, cut up <u>or</u><br>6 breast halves <u>or</u><br>10 chicken legs | Rinse with water. Shake off excess. Drop into dry mixture (2-3 pieces at a time) and shake to coat. |

2 Tbsp vegetable oil – Grease a 15x10 jelly roll pan with the oil.

Place floured chicken pieces skin side down in the pan. Do <u>not</u> crowd pieces.

Bake 425°, uncovered, for 30 min. Turn each piece over and bake 20 min longer or until juices are no longer pink when meat is pierced with a fork.

Note: For a more crisp and brown oven-fried chicken, use a very large cast iron skillet or a heavy dark-finish pizza pan.

# French Frying Batter

1 egg } Put into mixing bowl. Beat
1/3 c milk } with rotary beater (or use blender).

1 1/4 c Baker's "Flower" ♥ } Add and beat or
1/2 tsp salt } blend to mix thoroughly.

2/3 c milk - Gradually add second addition
of milk. Beat or blend to make
a smooth batter.

Blot with a paper towel to remove outside
moisture from food to be fried.

Shake in plain flour to coat each piece.

Dip in batter. Set pieces on a rack to
drip excess batter while grease heats.

Fry in <u>deep hot</u> (375°) fat until golden brown.

Drain on brown paper or on a rack set over
paper towels.

<u>Use batter for</u>: onion rings, cauliflower
pieces, whole cleaned shelled shrimp, scallops,
mushrooms, etc.

<u>Variation</u>: Add 2 Tbsp cornmeal with the
dry ingredients.

# Condiment Sauces

## Sweet & Sour Sauce

1/3 c catsup
1/3 c plum jelly
1 Tbsp prepared
  horseradish
} Heat, stirring constantly until jelly has melted.

## Hot Mustard Sauce

3 Tbsp dry mustard
2 Tbsp water
1 tsp soy sauce
} Mix until smooth.

## Tartar Sauce

1/2 c mayonnaise
2 Tbsp finely chopped
  pickle (dill or sweet)
1 tsp grated onion
} Combine ingredients, Refrigerate.

## Cocktail Sauce

1/2 c catsup
1 Tbsp prepared
  horseradish
1 tsp worcestershire sauce
} Mix together.

½ PINT        ½ PINT
ALE  ALE  ALE  ALE

# Potatoes

## Potato Pancakes

3 large baking potatoes - shred into a bowl of <u>cold</u> water.

2 eggs, beaten
1 small onion, grated
1 c dairy sour cream          } Stir in a mixing
2/3 c Baker's "Flower" ♥ /     bowl until well-
1/2 tsp salt                   blended.
1/4 tsp pepper

Vegetable oil - In a large skillet, add oil to 1/4" depth. Heat over med. high burner.

Drain potatoes. Remove excess water by squeezing in a clean linen towel. Stir into egg - sr. cream mixture.

Drop by tablespoonfuls into hot oil — flatten with a pancake turner.

Brown for 5-6 min. Turn over and brown second side. Drain on brown paper or on a cooling rack.   Serve hot.

# Golden Corn Bread

1 ¼ c Baker's "Flower" ♥ ⎞  Measure into mixing
1 c dry yellow cornmeal      ⎟  bowl.
1 tsp baking powder          ⎬  Rub with spoon or
1 ½ Tbsp sugar               ⎟  fingers to remove
½ tsp salt                   ⎠  "pebbles".

2 eggs, beaten ⎞  Combine egg and milk. Add to
1 c milk       ⎠  the dry ingredients. Stir
                  quickly to blend.

Put into a greased 9" round or 8" square pan.

Bake 375° 25-30 min or until golden brown
around the edges.

For corn muffins: Fill greased muffin tins
3/4 full. Bake 375° 15-20 min.

# Corn Bread Stuffing

2 c crumbled corn bread ⎞  Measure into mixing
2 c cubed dry bread     ⎠  bowl. Set aside.

½ c diced celery             ⎞
½ c diced onion              ⎬  Sauté until tender.
2 Tbsp butter or margarine   ⎠  in melted butter.

1 egg, beaten                    ⎞  Combine. Add cooked
1 c chicken broth                ⎟  celery and onion.
¼ tsp salt                       ⎬
⅛ tsp crumbled sage leaves       ⎟  Toss with the
⅛ tsp nutmeg                     ⎟  breads.
⅛ tsp pepper                     ⎠

Use to stuff 1 roasting chicken or put into
a buttered 1½ qt casserole dish. Cover loosely
with lid or foil.

Bake 325° for 30 min. Uncover, dot with butter.
Bake about 5 min longer.

Variations: Add ¼ tsp grated lemon rind, or
chopped cooked giblets or cooked, well-drained
sausage or about 2 Tbsp chopped pepperoni.

# Tamale Casserole

1 lb ground beef
1 med. onion, chopped fine
1 clove garlic, crushed
} Cook and stir in a skillet until meat is brown. <u>Drain.</u>

2 tsp chili powder
1 tsp salt
1/4 tsp black pepper
1 can (16 oz) tomatoes, not drained.
1/2 c sliced black olives
(1 Tbsp hot taco sauce)
} Stir with browned meat.
Put into an ungreased 8" sq or 9" round baking dish.

Top with cornmeal mixture:
    1 c yellow cornmeal
    1/2 c Baker's "flower" ♥
    1/4 tsp salt
} Blend dry ingredients.

    1 egg, beaten
    3/4 c milk
} Combine. Add to dry ingredients. Stir until well-mixed. Spoon batter over hot filling.

<u>Bake 375°</u> - 20 min. Top with 1 c shredded cheddar cheese. Bake 10 min longer.

# Basic White Sauce

2 Tbsp butter  - Melt in a small saucepan.

2 Tbsp Baker's "Flower" ♥ ⎫ stir into melted
¼ tsp salt                      ⎬ butter. Cook and stir
⅛ tsp pepper                 ⎭ until bubbly.

1 c milk · Add milk all at once. Cook and
              stir over med heat until sauce
              gets very hot and thickens.

Variations:

For a richer sauce, replace milk with cream.

Substitute 1c chicken broth or fish stock
for the milk.

Add chopped fresh parsley, garlic, onion,
nutmeg, parmesan cheese or other seasonings
to your taste.

For a CHEESE SAUCE, add ½ c grated cheese
to the hot, cooked white sauce. Serve over
cooked broccoli, cauliflower, onions, etc.

For a "HOLLANDAISE" SAUCE, add a few
tablespoons of the hot cooked sauce to
2 slightly beaten egg yolks. Mix together.
Return to remaining sauce in the pan
and stir to blend. Add 1 Tbsp lemon
juice and 4 Tbsp butter. Add the butter
1 Tbsp at a time and beat well after
each addition.

Serve your sauces over baked fish, chicken,
vegetables, cooked eggs, etc.

# Clam Chowder

4 slices bacon — Fry bacon in a 2 qt sauce-pan until crisp. Remove from pan and set aside.

1 med onion, chopped (½ c) — Add onion to bacon grease. Sauté until tender.

2 med potatoes, finely chopped ⎫ Add to onion. Stir.
1 med carrot, thinly sliced ⎭ Remove from heat.

2 cans minced clams — Drain liquid into measuring cup. <u>Add water to make 1 c.</u>

Add to vegetables. Bring to a boil. Reduce heat. <u>Cover</u> and simmer for 15 min or until vegetables are tender.

¼ c Baker's "Flower" ♥ ⎫ Add to vegetables. Stir
1 c milk ⎭ to blend.

2 c half and half ⎫ Add. Cook and stir over
¾ tsp salt ⎬ med heat, stirring
¼ tsp freshly ground pepper ⎭ constantly until chowder thickens and bubbles.

Add clams — heat through. Serve immediately topped with crumbled bacon.   4-6 servings

# Broccoli Chowder

1 - 10 oz pkg frozen — Cook as package directs.
  chopped broccoli    Drain.

¼ c butter or margarine ⎫ Sauté onion in melted
1 med onion, chopped ⎭ butter until tender.

¼ c Baker's "Flower" ♥ — Stir in. Cook till bubbly.

1 - 13½ oz can chicken broth — Add. Cook and stir until mixture comes to a boil.

1 c half and half ⎫ Add broccoli, half and half
¼ tsp salt ⎬ and seasonings. Cook till heated
⅛ tsp pepper ⎭ through but do <u>not</u> boil.

Serve immediately.    4-6 servings

# Beer-Cheese Soup

¼ c butter or margarine - Melt in 2 qt saucepan.

½ c finely chopped onions ⎫ Add vegetables.
⅓ c finely sliced carrots ⎬ Sauté for a couple
2 cloves garlic, crushed ⎭ of minutes.

⅓ c Baker's "Flower" ♥ ⎫ Stir in. Cook till bubbly.
⅛ tsp paprika ⎬ Remove from heat.
dash of nutmeg ⎭

1-10 oz can chicken broth ⎫ Add. Bring to a boil, Reduce
1 c flat beer ⎬ heat. Simmer for 15 min.

12 oz grated cheddar cheese - Add. Stir till cheese
                                    has melted.
1 c half and half    Add. Stir till thoroughly heated.
                         Do not boil.
Garnish with popcorn or croutons.
                            4-6 servings

# Potato Soup

3-4 med. potatoes, chopped ⎫ Put in a large pan.
1 c chopped onion ⎪ Cover. Bring to a
1 c diced celery ⎬ boil. Reduce heat,
½ tsp salt ⎪ Cook 20 min or
2 c water ⎭ until tender.

6 slices bacon - Fry in a separate pan or skillet
                     until crisp. Remove bacon.

3 Tbsp Baker's "Flower" ♥ - Add to bacon grease.
                             Cook and stir until
                             hot and bubbly.

2 c milk   Add milk. Cook and stir over
              med. heat until mixture just
              comes to a boil.

Add sauce to cooked (do not drain) vegetables.

Crumble bacon into the soup. Serve while hot.
                            4-6 servings

# Cheese Appetizers

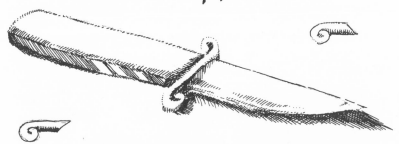

## Basic Cheese Pastry

2 Tbsp butter or
  margarine, softened
1 c shredded Monterrey Jack
  cheese (room temperature)
1 ⅓ c Baker's "Flower" ♥

} Stir or mix
  with hands
  to form dough.

Variations:

Shape into a thin log. <u>Chill</u> <u>until</u> <u>firm</u> (after wrapping in waxed paper or plastic wrap).
Slice ¼" thick. Place on baking sheet.
Sprinkle with paprika.
Bake 400° 7-10 min.

Roll into small balls. Place on a baking sheet.
Press a pecan half onto top of each.
Bake 400° -10 min.

Shape around pimento stuffed olive using only about 1 tsp dough.
Bake 400° 12-15 min.

Add 2 Tbsp finely chopped nuts before mixing.
Shape into small marble-sized balls. Use the bottom of a glass to flatten into wafers.
Bake 400° 7-10 min.

Add ½ tsp chili powder before mixing. Shape and bake as desired.

# Cheese Puffs

1 ½ c Baker's "Flower" ♥
1 c grated sharp cheddar
   cheese, room temperature
¼ c milk
2 Tbsp mayonnaise
¼ tsp onion powder

              } Blend in a
                mixing bowl.

Shape into very small (½") balls.

Put onto greased baking sheet.

Bake 400° - 10 min.

                 Makes 4 dozen

# Cornmeal Snack Crackers

6 Tbsp milk
2 Tbsp vegetable oil
1 tsp worcestershire sauce
1/4 tsp tobasco sauce
} Mix together in a measuring cup.

1 c cornmeal
2/3 c Baker's "Flower" ♥
1/4 tsp onion powder
} Measure dry ingredients into a mixing bowl.

Add liquids. Stir until dough gathers. Knead about 1 min. Add a few drops of milk if the dough is crumbly.

Divide dough into 2 parts. Shape one into a flattened rectangle. (Keep other half covered).

Place on a rimless greased cookie sheet. Cover with a large sheet of waxed paper. Using a rolling pin, flatten dough to 1/8" thick. Remove paper. Cut into 1" squares with pizza or pastry cutter. Sprinkle lightly with seasoned salt.

Bake 375° - 15 min.

# Stone-Ground Wheat Crackers

350°

| | |
|---|---|
| 1 c stone-ground whole wheat flour<br>2/3 c Baker's "Flower" ♥<br>1 Tbsp sugar<br>1/2 tsp salt | Stir dry ingredients together in a mixing bowl. |
| 1 Tbsp butter or margarine, softened<br>2/3 c buttermilk | Add to dry ingredients. Mix to make a stiff dough. |
| (2-4 Tbsp stone-ground whole wheat flour | Knead about 40 turns on flour dusted board. |

Divide dough into 2 parts. Shape each into a flattened rectangle. Sprinkle a rimless baking sheet with stone-ground flour. Place dough in the center and roll as thin as possible (less than 1/8") Dough should be fairly resistant. Using a pizza or pastry cutter, cut into small squares (1-1½").

Bake 350° (middle of oven) until crisp and slightly brown around the edges. If center crackers seem soft, remove baked outer crackers and return pan to oven. They will take from 15-25 min to bake.

# Cookies

# Tips on Cookie Making

Bake in pre-heated oven. Reduce temperature by 25 degrees if using glass baking pans. (For bars).

If cookie sheet is to be greased, use a solid vegetable shortening. A sheet of waxed paper is a great disposable "greaser".

Make cookies of uniform size so they'll all finish baking at the same time.

Place cookie sheets near center of oven when baking.

Always check at minimum baking time.

Remember that each cookie sheet will bake the cookies differently. A darker pan will cause quicker browning than one of a shiny metal.

Immediately remove cookies to a wire rack for cooling unless directions state otherwise. Use a wide spatula or pancake turner for easy removal.

Store cooled crisp cookies in a loosely covered container. Store cooled soft cookies in a tightly covered container.

## For rolled cookies

If dough has been chilled, roll only a portion — keep remainder chilled.

Sprinkle rolling surface with flour. Use sparingly but use enough to keep dough from sticking. Also, dust rolling pin or top of dough with flour.

Roll to an even thickness so all cookies will take an equal amount of baking time.

Dip cookie cutter into flour to prevent sticking. Cut close together.

Lift onto baking sheet with a spatula.

113

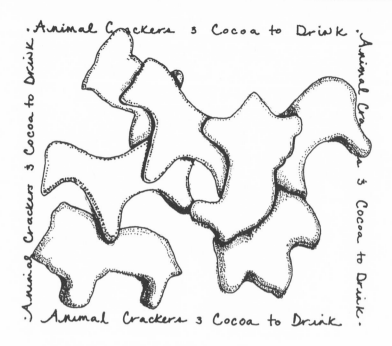

# "Animal Crackers"

400°

| | |
|---|---|
| ½ c brown sugar, packed | Measure Into mixing bowl. stir to blend. |
| 2 Tbsp light corn syrup | |
| 2 Tbsp milk | |
| 1 tsp lemon extract | |
| 1 tsp vanilla | |

2 ¼ c Baker's "Flower" ♥ - Add in <u>three</u> <u>parts</u>.

Use hands, if necessary, to mix in the final addition. Gather into a ball. Divide in 2 parts.

Roll on a floured board to ⅛" thick. Cut with floured tiny cookie cutters.

Place on a lightly greased cookie sheet.

Bake 400° 6-8 min until lightly browned.

# Apricot Bars

375°

3/4 c Baker's "Flower" ♥  ⎫  Stir to blend
3/4 c flour                ⎬  in a mixing
1 c brown sugar, packed    ⎭  bowl.

1/2 c butter or      – Chop butter into several
  margarine, firm      pieces. Cut in with
                       pastry blender or work in
                       with fingers to form a
                       crumb mixture.

1 1/4 c quick-       – Add oatmeal to above
  cooking oats         mixture. Toss to blend.

Reserve 1 1/2 c crumb mixture to sprinkle
over the top. Press remainder evenly
into a greased 8" sq. pan.

Spread 3/4 c apricot preserves carefully
over the pressed layer.

Cover evenly with reserved crumbs – pat
lightly to firm.

Bake 375° 30-35 min or until golden brown.
Cool before cutting.

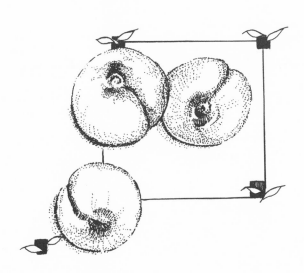

# Arrowroot 'Crackers'

350°

1/3 c butter or margarine, softened
1/4 c sugar } Cream together with a large mixing spoon.

2 Tbsp milk - Stir in to blend.

3/4 c Baker's "flower" ♥ - Add and mix well.

3/4 c corn starch - Add to dough. Blend thoroughly. Cover and <u>chill</u> till firm.

On a floured surface, roll dough to 1/8" thick. Cut with a 2" biscuit cutter.

Place on a lightly <u>floured</u> cookie sheet. Prick each cookie 3 times with tines of fork.

Bake 350° 15-20 min in middle of oven until lightly browned.

2-2 1/2 doz.

# Baker's Brownies

350°

1 c sugar
2/3 c flour
¼ c Baker's "flower" ♥
¼ c dry cocoa
} Blend in a bowl until well-mixed. Press or rub back of spoon against sides of bowl.

½ c butter or margarine, melted and slightly cooled
2 eggs
1 tsp vanilla
} Add to dry ingredients. Stir till well-mixed.

(½ c chopped nuts) - (Add nuts)

Grease bottom only of an 8" sq. pan. Spread mixture to ¼" from the edges. (This helps prevent "creeping" up the sides.)

Bake 350° 25-30 min. Cool in pan.

## Cocoa Frosting

1¼ c powdered sugar
3 Tbsp dry cocoa
} Sift if lumpy. Stir till blended.

2 Tbsp butter or margarine, melted
1½ Tbsp hot tap water
½ tsp vanilla
} Add to cocoa-powdered sugar mixture, adding water gradually to desired thickness. Beat until smooth.

Spread over cooled brownies.

Alright! Who took the last brownie?

COCOA

# Chewy Fudge Brownies

325°

2 sq unsweetened
chocolate ( 1 oz each)  } Melt together. Cool
1/4 c butter or            } slightly.
margarine

1 c sugar              } Stir into melted
1/3 c Baker's "Flower" ♥ } chocolate.

1/3 c flour - Add and blend thoroughly.

1 egg <u>plus</u> 1 egg yolk } Add. Stir vigorously
1 tsp vanilla             } until well-mixed.

1/2 c chopped nuts - Stir in nuts.

Spread evenly in a greased (bottom only)
9" sq pan leaving a 1/4" space around edge.
Bake 325° 25-30 min.

# Fudge Frosting

1 sq unsweetened ) Bring to a boil in a small
chocolate (1oz)  ( saucepan. Stir frequently
3 Tbsp milk      ( to prevent scorching. Remove
1/4 c sugar      ) from heat.

2 Tbsp butter    ) Add immediately to hot mixture
1/2 tsp vanilla  ( Begin with 1 c powdered sugar-
Powdered sugar   ) add and stir till smooth. Add
                   enough more to make a thin
                   frosting. Let set till cooled.
                   Beat again. Add more sugar
                   if needed. Spread on cooled
                   brownies.

Unsweetened Chocolate

# Butterscotch Squares

350°

3 Tbsp butter or
  margarine, softened
7/8 c brown sugar, packed        Stir together
1 egg                            until well-mixed.
1 tsp vanilla
1/3 c Baker's "Flower" ♥

1/2 c flour    - Add flour. Blend thoroughly.

1/2 c chopped pecans  - Stir in nuts.
  or walnuts

Spread dough in a greased (bottom only) 8"sq
pan — leaving a 1/4"-1/2" space around the edges.

Bake 350° about 25 min.

Roll cooled bars in powdered sugar, if desired.


Variation: 1/2 c chocolate chips or coconut
can be substituted for the nuts.

# Butter Wafers

350°

3/4 c butter or
 margarine, softened
3/4 c powdered sugar
2 Tbsp brown sugar
1/3 c Baker's "Flower"

} Measure into mixing bowl. Stir vigorously until well-blended.

1 1/3 c flour - Add about 1/2 c at a time. Blend well after each addition.

Shape into small balls (3/4" diameter). Place on ungreased cookie sheet. Use a glass with a design on the bottom to flatten the cookies. Dip glass bottom into flour and tap off excess between each imprint.

Bake 350° 10-12 min or until outer edges are beginning to brown.

This dough must be firm enough to hold its shape while baking. You might want to try a test cookie. Add a bit of extra flour, if necessary.

4 doz cookies

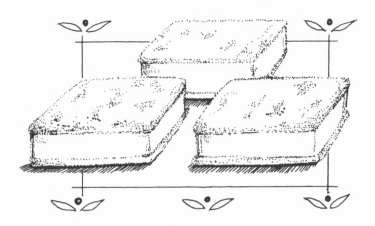

# Cheesecake Bars

350°

| 1¼ c Baker's "Flower" ♥ | Blend to make a |
| 3 Tbsp butter or | crumb mixture. |
| margarine, softened | <u>Remove 1 cup.</u> |
| ½ c brown sugar, packed | Pat remainder into |
| ¼ tsp cinnamon | an 8" sq pan (not greased) |

Bake 350° - middle oven rack - 9 min or until lightly browned.

Prepare filling:

1 - 8 oz pkg cream cheese, — Whip cheese with
    softened              a large mixing
¼ c sugar             spoon until fluffy.
1 egg         Add to the cream cheese
            and stir until well-blended.

2 Tbsp milk - Add gradually. Mix well.
2 Tbsp lemon juice - blend in.

Spread cream cheese mixture over partially baked crust. <u>Sprinkle</u> with <u>reserved</u> <u>crumbs</u>.

Bake 350° 20-25 min longer or until golden brown. Cool in pan. Cut into bars.
(Store in refrigerator).

# Chocolate Chip Cookies

375°

¼ c butter or
  margarine, softened
½ c sugar
½ c brown sugar, packed   } Using a large spoon,
                            beat together
                            in a mixing bowl.
1 egg
1 Tbsp milk

1 ¾ c Baker's "Flower" ♥  } Add to the above
¼ tsp baking soda          } mixture. Stir till well-
                             blended.

1- 6 oz pkg chocolate chips - Add chips (and
(½ c chopped nuts)            nuts). Mix well.

Drop 2" apart on ungreased cookie sheet.
Bake 375° 8-10 min or until lightly browned.

Cool slightly before removing from pan to rack.

(Increase Baker's "Flower" 2-4 Tbsp for a
more rounded cookie.)

# Chewy Chocolate Chip Cookies

1½ c brown sugar
¼ c butter or
  margarine, softened    } Using a large spoon,
                          beat together in
                          a mixing bowl.
2 eggs
2 Tbsp honey

2 ½ c Baker's "Flower" ♥ } Add. Stir till
½ tsp baking soda        } well-blended.

1- 6 oz pkg chocolate chips - Add chips (and
(⅔ c chopped nuts)           nuts). Mix well.

Drop by spoonfuls onto ungreased baking sheet.

Bake 375° 8-10 min until lightly browned.

Cool slightly before removing from pan to
cooling rack.

# Soft Chocolate Drop Cookies

350°

2 - 1 oz sqs. Unsweetened ⎫ Melt together.
    chocolate.                ⎬ Cool slightly. Set aside.
3 Tbsp butter               ⎭

2½ c Baker's "Flower" ♥ ⎫ Measure into a mixing
1 c brown sugar          ⎬ bowl. Rub with fingers
                          ⎭ or back of spoon to
                            blend.

1 egg            ⎫ Add along with the melted
1 tsp vanilla    ⎬ chocolate and <u>half</u> (6 Tbsp) of
                 ⎭ the buttermilk to the dry mixture.
3/4 c buttermilk. Beat together with a large
mixing spoon to make a fluffy
smooth batter.

Add remaining buttermilk in 2 parts and mix
well after each addition.

Drop by spoonfuls onto a greased and flour-
dusted cookie sheet.

Bake 350° 10-12 min or until centers spring
back when touched lightly. Cool on rack.
Frost if desired.

Variation: substitute plain milk for buttermilk.

# Mocha Frosting

1¼ c powdered sugar  ⎫ Blend together (sift
1 Tbsp cocoa          ⎬ or stir)
1 tsp instant coffee  ⎭
   powder

2 Tbsp butter or         ⎫ Add. Beat with a
   margarine, softened   ⎬ mixing spoon
2 Tbsp milk              ⎭ until smooth.
1 tsp vanilla

TIME    TEA TIME    TEA TIME    TEA

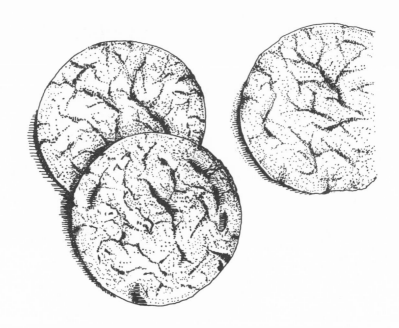

# Chocolate Mint Snappers

350°

| | |
|---|---|
| 5 Tbsp butter or margarine, softened<br>1 c sugar<br>1 egg | Stir with a large mixing spoon until well-beaten. |
| ¼ c light corn syrup<br>2 oz unsweetened chocolate, melted<br>½ tsp mint extract | Add to the above mixture. Chocolate should be slightly cooled. Mix well. |
| 2⅓ c Baker's "flower" ♥<br>1 tsp cinnamon<br>½ tsp baking soda | Add. Stir until thoroughly blended. Refrigerate to firm dough. |

Shape into 1" balls. Roll in granulated sugar.

Place on lightly greased cookie sheet.

Bake 350° – 15 min

3½ doz cookies

# Cocoa Sandwich Cookies

400°

1 1/2 c Baker's "Flower" ♥  } Rub to blend in
1 c sugar                    } a mixing bowl.
2/3 c cocoa

1/2 c butter or              } Add slightly cooled
  margarine, melted          } melted butter, egg and
1 egg                        } water to cocoa mixture.
1 Tbsp water (or rum)        } Stir vigorously until
                               thoroughly blended.

1/2 c flour — Add 1/4 c at a time. Stir until
             well·mixed.

Shape into 3/4" balls. Place on ungreased
cookie sheet. Flatten to 1/8" with palm of hand
or use a drinking glass with a bottom design. Dip
the glass in sugar before stamping each time.

Bake 400° 8·9 min.

                    About 4 doz cookies


Match into pairs. Spread one side with:
    2 c powdered sugar
    1 Tbsp solid vegetable shortening  } Add only enough
    1/2 tsp vanilla                    } milk to make a
    2 · 3 Tbsp milk                    } fluffy frosting.

Top with 2nd cookie — 24 sandwiches

❦ 125

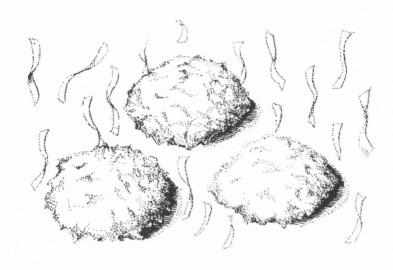

# Coconut Macaroons

325°

3 egg whites } Beat till stiff but not dry.
⅛ tsp salt }

1 c powdered sugar - Add gradually beating
                        to stiff peak stage.

1 tsp vanilla   - Add and blend well.

3 c flaked coconut        } Gently fold into
6 Tbsp Baker's "Flower" ❤ } the meringue
                            mixture.

Drop by teaspoonfuls onto greased and flour
dusted cookie sheet.

Bake 325° 15-20 min or until lightly browned.

Remove to a cooling rack. When cool,
store in a tightly covered container.

2½ doz.

# Gingersnaps

375°

2 Tbsp butter or
  margarine, softened
1 c brown sugar, packed
2 Tbsp molasses
1 egg

} Put into a mixing bowl. Beat with a spoon until well-blended.

2 ½ c Baker's "Flower" ♥
1 tsp cinnamon
½ tsp ginger
¼ tsp cloves
¼ tsp baking soda

} Combine dry ingredients <u>before</u> adding to above mixture. Then, add and stir until thoroughly mixed.

Cover and refrigerate to firm dough.

Shape into 3/4" balls. Place on a lightly greased cookie sheet.

Bake 375° ·10 min.    About 4 doz cookies

# Gingerbread Cookies

375°

½ c butter or
  margarine, softened
1 c sugar          } Beat together with
1 egg              } a large mixing spoon.
2 Tbsp corn syrup
1 tsp orange extract

2 c Baker's "Flower" ♥ } Add. Stir until
2 tsp cinnamon          } well-blended.
1 tsp ginger
½ tsp cloves

1 c flour · Add in three additions. Stir each
            time until thoroughly mixed. (Use
            hands if necessary).
Wrap and refrigerate to firm dough.

Roll on a lightly floured surface to about ¼"
thickness. Cut with floured cookie cutters.
Place 1 inch apart on ungreased baking sheet.

Bake 375° 7-10 min for a med-size cookie.

# Home-Style Graham Crackers

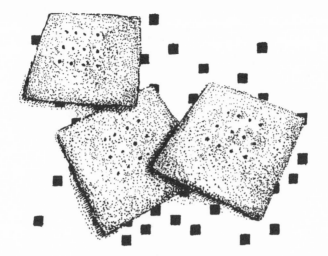

325°

¼ c butter or
   margarine, softened
¼ c brown sugar, packed
¼ c honey
¼ c water
} Stir together with a large mixing spoon.

1 ¼ c Baker's "Flower" ♥
1 tsp cinnamon
½ tsp salt
} Add. Stir till well-blended.

1 ½ c whole wheat flour - stir in ½ c at a time
                            (Use hands, if necessary)

Divide dough into 2 parts. Keep one part covered.

Press the uncovered half into a flattened rectangle. Put onto greased rimless cookie sheet. Cover with a large sheet of waxed paper. Roll to ⅛" thick.

Remove waxed paper. Using a pizza cutter, cut into 2½"-3" squares. Prick each cookie 3 times with tines of fork.

Bake 325° on lower middle oven rack for about 25 min. <u>Check</u> <u>at</u> <u>20</u> <u>min</u>. Remove cookies around the edges if brown. Return remainder to oven to finish baking. Cool baked cookies on wire rack. (Repeat with 2nd part of dough).

# Fruit-Filled Bars

1/4 c butter or
  margarine, softened
1/2 c brown sugar, packed
1 egg white, unbeaten
1 tsp vanilla
1/4 c Baker's "Flower" ♥
      } Beat together with a large mixing spoon.

1 c flour - Add. Blend thoroughly.

1/2 c oatmeal — Add dry oats. Stir till well-mixed.

Gather together. Shape into a log. Cut in half.

Press one of the halves into a greased 8" sq pan. Spread with fruit filling.

Shape the second half into a flattened square. Roll between 2 sheets of waxed paper to 8" sq. Remove top sheet. Invert over fruit filling — carefully remove paper. Trim to fit. Prick well with fork tines.

Bake 350° 18-20 min until lightly browned.

Let cool about 10 min before removing from pan to cut into bars.

## FRUIT FILLING FOR COOKIES

1 c dried fruit (dates, raisins, apricots, figs, or any combination — Cut fruit into small pieces. Cover with boiling water. Soak for 10 min. Drain.

1 Tbsp honey or light corn syrup
1 Tbsp butter
2 Tbsp water
    } Combine with fruit in a small saucepan. Cook and stir over low heat until a thick paste forms. Add more water, if needed.

(1/4 c finely chopped nuts) (Add nuts). Cool mixture before spreading over BARS.

# Granola Bars

325°

3 Tbsp butter or
   margarine, softened
1 c brown sugar, packed
1/2 c peanut butter
1/4 c honey
1 egg
1/2 c Baker's "Flower" ❤
1 tsp cinnamon

} Measure into mixing bowl. Stir till well-blended.

2 c dry rolled oats
   (reserve 1/4 c)
1/2 c coconut

} stir in coconut and 1 3/4 c <u>only</u> of dry oats (oatmeal).

Scrape sticky dough onto center of a <u>greased</u> and <u>wax paper</u> lined 13x9 pan. Grease both the bottom of the pan <u>and</u> the top of the paper.

Press with back of mixing spoon to partially flatten, Sprinkle with <u>reserved oats</u>. Cover with another sheet of waxed paper, press and smooth with open hands to flatten dough evenly. Remove paper.

Bake 325° 35-40 min or until center is "set". Let stand 10-15 min. Remove from pan. <u>Peel off paper</u>. Set on cooling rack, Cut cooled bars on a board.    Makes 27 bars

· HONEY · PEANUT BUTTER ·

COCONUT · OATMEAL

OATMEAL · COCONUT

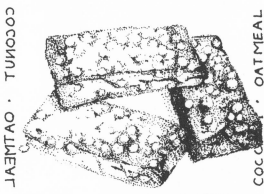

· HONEY · PEANUT BUTTER ·

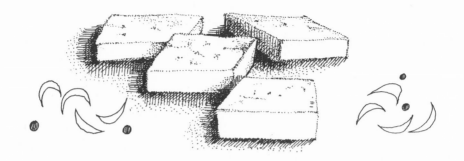

# Lemon Bars

350°

3/4 c flour
1/3 c Baker's "Flower" ♥  } Stir together
1/4 c powdered sugar       in a small
                           mixing bowl.

6 Tbsp butter or          } Add to dry ingredients.
  margarine, melted          Mix well. Press onto
                             bottom of an 8" sq lightly
                             greased pan.
Bake 350° 15-20 min or until slightly browned.

While the crust is baking, prepare the
filling:

    3 Tbsp Baker's "Flower" ♥ } Measure into
    7/8 c sugar                 mixing bowl.
Rub back of spoon against the mixture
to blend thoroughly.

    2 eggs
    3 Tbsp lemon juice        } Add to sugar-
    1 tsp grated lemon rind     flour mixture.
                                Stir vigorously
                                till blended.

Pour over <u>hot</u> baked crust. Bake 350°
for 20 min.

Cool. Store in refrigerator.

Before serving, sprinkle with powdered sugar.

Cut into 16 squares.

# Oatmeal Cookies

350°

½ c butter or
  margarine, softened          ⎫
½ c sugar                      ⎬  Stir together in a
2/3 c brown sugar, packed      ⎭  mixing bowl.
1 egg
1 tsp vanilla

1 c plus 2 Tbsp Baker's "flower" ♥ ⎫  Add. Stir till
¼ tsp salt                         ⎬  well-blended.
½ tsp cinnamon                     ⎭
¼ tsp nutmeg

2½ c quick oats (dry)      Stir in oatmeal.

Drop by spoonfuls onto a greased cookie sheet.
Bake 350° 12-15 min.

Makes 4 doz 3" cookies

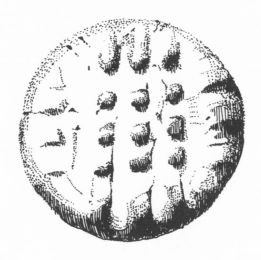

# Peanut Butter Cookies

375°

¼ c butter or
  margarine, softened
½ c peanut butter          } Stir together in a
½ c brown sugar, packed      mixing bowl until
½ c sugar                    blended.
1 egg

1 ⅔ c Baker's "Flower" ♥  - Add. Stir vigorously
                                       until well-mixed.

Shape into small balls (1"). Place on lightly
greased cookie sheet.

Dip fork tines in flour and press into cookie
dough to form a criss-cross design.

Bake 375° 8-10 min. Watch closely — do not
overbake — these burn quickly.

                          About 40 - 2½" cookies

# Peanut Butter-Chocolate Chip Cookies

3/4 c smooth peanut butter
1/4 c butter or
  margarine, softened
1/2 c sugar
1/2 c brown sugar
        } combine in a
          mixing bowl.
          Stir till creamy.

1/4 c milk
1 egg
  } Add. Stir till blended.

1 3/4 c Baker's "Flower" ♥ - Add in 3 parts.
                       Mix thoroughly.

1 - 6 oz. pkg chocolate chips - Add chips to the
                            dough.

Drop by spoonfuls onto ungreased baking sheet.
Bake 350° 10-12 min.

                  4 doz 2 1/4" cookies

# Old World Spice Cookies

400°

½ c brown sugar, packed
⅓ c light molasses
¼ c milk
1 tsp grated lemon rind
} Stir together in a mixing bowl.

3 c Baker's "Flower" ♥
1 tsp cinnamon, ¼ tsp cloves,
  ¼ tsp ginger
} Stir together <u>before</u> adding to the above mixture. Add; blend well.

Wrap in plastic wrap. <u>Chill</u> to firm dough.

Roll out half of the dough on a floured board to about ⅛" thickness. Dip cookie cutter in flour as necessary.

Bake on a lightly greased cookie sheet - 400° for 7-10 min. Cool before glazing.

### WHITE GLAZE FOR COOKIES

1 egg white - Beat until foamy (first stage).
1 c powdered sugar - Add gradually to make a <u>thin</u> icing. You may need additional powdered sugar.

This will dry to a hard glaze.

# Polka-Dot Candy Cookies

375°

1/3 c butter or
  margarine, softened
2/3 c brown sugar, packed
1/3 c sugar
1 egg
1 tsp vanilla
} Measure into mixing bowl. Stir vigorously with a large mixing spoon until well-blended.

1 3/4 c Baker's "Flower" ♥
1/4 tsp baking soda
} Add. Mix thoroughly.

3/4 c dry oatmeal — Stir into dough until blended.

1 c candy-coated
  plain chocolate candies — Add 1/2 c only. Stir.

Drop onto ungreased cookie sheet. Decorate tops of each with remaining 1/2 c candy (use 2-3 per cookie)

Bake 375° 10 min or until golden brown. Let set a minute or two before removing from pan.

2 doz - 3½" cookies

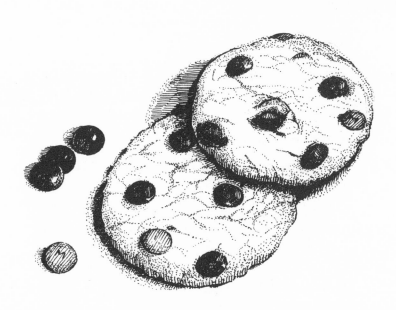

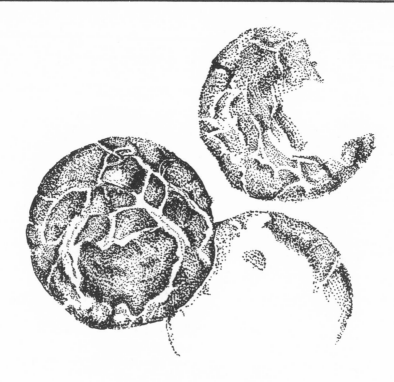

# Snickerdoodles

400°

⅓ c butter or
  margarine, softened
1 c sugar
1 egg
1 tsp vanilla
} Beat with a mixing spoon until well-blended.

2 ½ c Baker's "Flower" ♥
½ tsp baking soda
} stir together before adding to above ingredients.

Combine both and mix thoroughly.

Shape rounded teaspoonfuls into balls.
Roll gently in sugar-cinnamon mixture.
(2 Tbsp sugar mixed with 2 tsp cinnamon).

Place 2" apart on ungreased baking sheet.

Bake 400° 8-10 min or until lightly browned.

      About 3 doz - 2½" cookies

# Snowball Cookies

375°

3/4 c butter or<br>
  margarine, softened } With a mixing spoon,<br>
1/3 c powdered sugar } beat together until<br>
1 tsp vanilla } light and fluffy.

1/2 c Baker's "Flower" ♥ - Add. Stir in until<br>
                well-blended.

1 1/2 c flour - Gradually add remaining flour.<br>
      It will seem dry, but it will<br>
      work in — you may need to<br>
      use your hands.

3/4 c finely chopped nuts - Stir into the dough.

Shape into 1" balls. Place about 1" apart
on an ungreased baking sheet.

Bake 375° 12-15 min - Cookies should be
set and just slightly browned.

Remove to a cooling rack. Roll in powdered
sugar while warm.

Cool. Roll again.

About 4 doz

# Toffee Bars

325°

3/4 c brown sugar, packed  
1/3 c sugar  
1/2 c butter or  
   margarine, softened  
1 egg yolk  
1 tsp vanilla  
1/2 c Baker's "Flower" ♥

Stir together in a mixing bowl until thoroughly blended.

1 c flour   - Add flour in 3 parts. It will seem dry, but it will work together.

1 c coarsely chopped   - Add 1/2 c of the almonds almonds, divided    to the dough. Mix together.

Pat into a lightly greased 11 x 8 pan — leaving 1/4-1/2" space between edges of dough and sides of pan. Prick generously with fork tines.

Bake 325° 23-28 min or until puffy and golden brown. Remove from oven. Let set for a couple of minutes.

Sprinkle with:  
      6 oz chocolate chips  
Let stand till softened. Spread evenly. Quickly scatter <u>remaining</u> <u>1/2 c nuts</u>. Cut while warm.

# Rich Sugar Cookies

350°

1/2 c butter or
  margarine, softened } Cream together with
1 c sugar            a mixing spoon.

1 egg
1 tsp almond flavoring } Add to creamed mixture.
1/2 tsp vanilla       Stir vigorously till
                  well-mixed.

3 c Baker's "Flower" ♥   Add. Mix till thoroughly
                         blended.

Cover and refrigerate for 2 hrs before rolling.

Roll on a lightly floured board to 1/8" thickness.
Cut into 2 1/2" rounds with a cookie cutter.
Put on an ungreased baking sheet.

Bake 350° 8-10 min. Remove from pan to
cooling rack. Sprinkle with sugar while hot.

                   About 5 doz.

# Old-Time Sugar Cookies

375°

3 Tbsp butter or
  margarine, softened } Measure into mixing bowl.
1/2 c sugar         Stir with a large spoon
1 egg              until well-mixed.
1 tsp vanilla

2 1/3 c Baker's "Flower" ♥ - Add 1 1/3 c only to
  (add in 2 parts)        above mixture. Stir
                    till well-blended.
Add remaining ♥, Stir, or use hands if it
is difficult to blend.

Gather together. Shape into a ball, Chill
in refrigerator to firm dough.

Roll 1/8"-1/4" thick. on a floured board. Cut
with floured cookie cutter. Put on a lightly
greased baking sheet.

Bake 375° 6-10 min. Amount of cookies and
length of baking time will vary according
to size and thickness of cookie.

# Wheat Cookies

350°

3/4 c sugar
1/3 c butter or
   margarine, softened
1 tsp vanilla
1 tsp vinegar
2 eggs
1 1/4 c Baker's "Flower" ♥

Beat together with a large mixing spoon until well-blended.

1 1/2 c whole wheat flour
1 tsp cinnamon
1/4 tsp baking soda

Mix together _before_ combining with the above ingredients. Stir till thoroughly mixed. _Chill until firm._

Roll on a well floured board to 1/8" thick.
Put on a lightly greased baking sheet.
Bake 350° 12-15 min.

These cookies can be sprinkled with sugar and cinnamon _or_ filled with preserves or pastry fillings (folded and sealed) _before_ baking.

Cakes

# Cake Making Information

1. Always <u>preheat</u> <u>oven</u>. Lower oven temperature by $\overline{25°}$ if using a glass baking pan.

2. To prepare pan, or pans, grease bottom and lower ridge only — do not grease sides. Dust with flour, tap out excess.

3. Be sure to use correct size of pan - use size specified or an equivalent.

4. Measure accurately. Spoon dry ingredients into nested measuring cups. Level with a straight edged spatula or knife. Use marked glass measuring cups for liquids – check at eye level.

5. Use large eggs in these recipes.

6. Do not use whipped butter or margarine. These recipes have been tested for stick type butter and margarine.

7. Blend on low speed to moisten; then beat as directed. Feed batter towards beaters to increase volume and to create a smooth batter.

8. Put into prepared pans.

9. Bake on center rack of oven.

10. Set timer for minimum baking time. Test center of cake with a wooden pick or as recipe directs.

11. Let set in pan for 8-10 min. before removing from pan to cooling rack. Slide a knife around the edges to loosen.

12. Cool before frosting (unless recipe indicates otherwise).

# One Layer Basic Cake

350°                                             *(elec mixer)*

1⅓ c Baker's "Flower" ♥ } Stir together.
⅔ c sugar

1½ Tbsp butter or
   margarine, softened
½ c milk
1 egg
} Add and blend on low speed just to moisten. Beat on med speed for 2 min while pushing batter towards beaters.

Put into a greased and floured (bottom only) 8"sq or 8" or 9" round layer pan.

Bake 350° - 30-35 min or until a wooden pick inserted in the center comes out clean.

## TO BEAT BY HAND

Use ingredients as above — however, milk and egg will be added separately.

Add only 6 Tbsp milk to the dry ingredients. Beat with a large spoon until the batter is smooth and fluffy.

Add remainder of milk in 2 parts- 1 Tbsp at a time. Beat thoroughly after each addition.

Add egg and beat about 100 strokes.

Bake as above. Top with BROILED COCONUT-PECAN TOPPING or as desired.

VARIATIONS:    UPSIDE-DOWN CAKE
                      MARBLE CAKE

# Broiled Coconut-Pecan Topping

Make a 1-layer BASIC CAKE. Top while still warm. Brown under the broiler.

| | |
|---|---|
| 1/4 c butter or margarine, melted<br>1/2 c brown sugar, packed<br>3 Tbsp cream or milk<br>1/2 c shredded coconut<br>1/4 c chopped pecans | Mix together. Spread on slightly warm cake. Broil till bubbly and lightly browned. |

Set cake about 5" below broiler heating element for about 3 min. Watch closely to prevent burning.

# Marble Cake

½ sq chocolate — melt chocolate.
(unsweetened)

1 Tbsp warm water } Add to melted chocolate.
⅛ tsp baking soda } Stir together. Set aside.

Prepare BASIC CAKE batter.

Using about 2/3 of the batter, drop by spoonfuls into separated spots into a greased and floured 8" sq. or 9" round cake pan.

Add the prepared chocolate to the remaining batter and blend on low speed till thoroughly mixed.

Spoon chocolate batter between the light batter. Cut through with a table knife to produce a marbled effect.

# Upside Down Cake

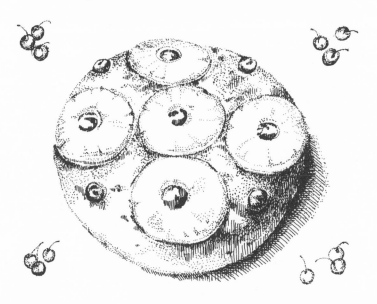

Prepare the pan with fruit before mixing the BASIC CAKE batter. Use a 9" skillet with oven-proof handle or an 8" sq cake pan.

1/4 c butter or margarine, melted — cover bottom of pan with melted butter.

1/2 c brown sugar, packed — Sprinkle evenly over the butter.

1- 8 1/4 oz can sliced pineapple, well-drained — Arrange 4 slices of pineapple into a design.

Maraschino cherries — Add cherry decoration, if desired.

Mix batter. Spoon over the fruit.

Bake 350° 40-45 min or until wooden pick comes out clean. Invert onto heat-proof plate and let pan set over it for a few minutes before removing. Serve warm with whipped cream.

Substitute canned pineapple with canned peach slices, if desired.

# Devil's Food Cake

350° (elec mixer)

2 c Baker's "Flower" ♥  ⎫
1 1/3 c sugar              ⎬  stir dry ingredients
1/2 c cocoa               ⎪  to blend.
1/2 tsp baking soda      ⎭

2 Tbsp butter or          ⎫  Add to dry ingredients.
  margarine, softened     ⎬  Blend on low speed to
1 c milk                  ⎭  moisten. Beat on med.
                              speed scraping bottom
                              and sides of bowl for 1 1/2 min.

2 eggs. Add. Blend quickly on low speed. Beat
        on med speed for 1 1/2 min.

Put into greased and floured 13x9 pan or 2 8"or
9" round layer pans.
Bake 350° – layers 30-35 min
            oblong - 35-40 min
when done, wooden pick should come out clean
and center should spring back when lightly touched.
set on a cooling rack for about 10 min
before removing from pan.

Variation: Replace milk with buttermilk.

# Quick Cocoa Icing

1 1/2 c powdered sugar
3 Tbsp cocoa
} Sift or stir until well-blended.

3 Tbsp butter or margarine, softened
2 Tbsp milk
1/2 tsp vanilla
} Add to powdered sugar mixture. Beat with a spoon until smooth and fluffy.

Frosts 1 layer.

# Creamy Fudge Frosting

1/3 c butter or margarine
2 sq (2 oz) unsweetened chocolate
} Melt in double boiler over hot water.

1/4 c evaporated milk (or cream) — Add and stir with melted chocolate. Remove from heat.

1/2 tsp vanilla
3 1/2 - 4 c powdered sugar (sift if lumpy)
} Add. Stir until smooth and creamy. Cool. Beat well before frosting the cake.

Enough for a 2 layer cake.

# Yellow Cake

(elec. mixer)

2 ¾ c Baker's "Flower" ♥ } Stir together in
1 ½ c sugar                 } larger mixer bowl.

¼ c butter or            ) Add to dry ingredients.
  margarine, softened  ) Blend on low to moisten.
1 c milk                 ) Beat on med. speed for
1 tsp vanilla            ) 1½ min. scraping bottom
                            and sides of bowl.

3 eggs  - Add eggs. Blend quickly; then beat
            on med speed 1½ min. longer

Put batter in a 13x9x2  or 2 round layer
pans (8" or 9") which have been greased and
floured on pan bottoms only.

Bake 350°  40-45 min - oblong
           35-40 min. - layers

Test with wooden pick Cool 8-10 min before
removing from pan to cooling rack.

cupcakes: Fill paper-lined muffin tins
          half full. Bake 18-20 min
                        About 3 doz

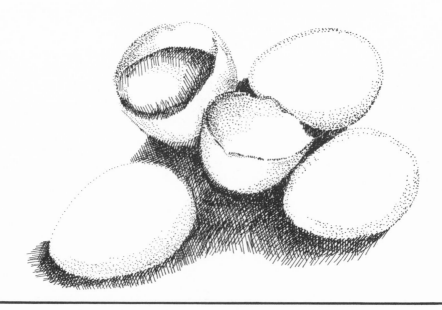

# Creamy Butter Icing

1 egg white     - Beat until foamy (like soap suds).

3 c powdered sugar
2 Tbsp butter, softened
2 Tbsp white solid
   vegetable shortening
2 Tbsp milk
1 tsp vanilla

} Add. Beat until smooth
and creamy.
Add extra powdered
sugar if needed.

Frosts a large cake or 2 layers.

# Wedding Cake Frosting

3 c powdered sugar
1/4 c butter or margarine,
   softened
3-4 Tbsp milk
1 tsp vanilla

} Measure ingredients
and put into a mixing
bowl. Begin with 3 Tbsp
milk - add more if needed.
Beat until light and
creamy with a mixing
spoon or electric mixer.

Frosts a large cake or 2 layers.

# White Cake

350°                                        (elec mixer)

1 1/3 c Baker's "Flower" ♥ } Stir together in smaller
3/4 c sugar                       } bowl of elec. mixer.

1 Tbsp butter or            ⎫ Add to the dry ingredients.
   margarine, softened   ⎪ Blend on low speed to
6 Tbsp milk                   ⎬ moisten. Beat on med speed
1/2 tsp vanilla                ⎭ 1 1/2 min while scraping bowl.

2 egg whites  - Add. Blend on low speed. Beat
                        on med speed 1 1/2 min longer
                        scraping bowl occasionally.

Put into prepared pan. (Grease and flour only
the bottom of an 8" sq or 9" round pan)

Bake 350° 30·35 min on middle oven rack
until cake tests done with a wooden pick.

Cool 8·10 min before removing from pan to
cooling rack.

Double above recipe for a 2·layer or oblong
cake. Bake 1 large cake 35·40 min.

ANNIVE̶̶̶ · WEDDING · BON VOYAGE
WELCOME HOME · HAPPY BIRTHDAY

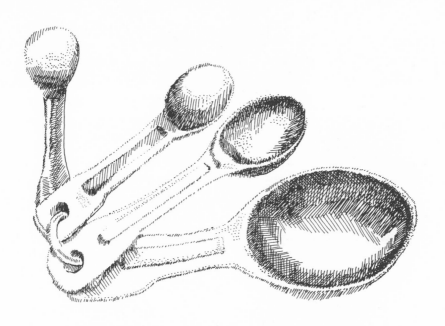

# Velvet Cream Frosting

1 c sugar           } Combine in a
2/3 c Baker's "Flower" ♥ } saucepan.

1 c milk      Add gradually to the dry
ingredients and mix well.
Cook and stir over med. heat
until mixture boils for 1 min.
Cool. Then, refrigerate until
well-chilled.

3/4 c butter or
margarine, softened    Cream in smaller bowl
of elec. mixer on med.
speed until light and
fluffy. Gradually add
cooled mixture while
beat on med-high speed.

1 tsp vanilla     Add and blend well.

Frosts a large cake or 2 layers.

# Spice Cake

350°                                              (elec. mixer)

2 3/4 c Baker's "Flower" ♥ ⎫
1 1/2 c sugar              ⎪  Stir together in
1 tsp cinnamon            ⎬  the larger
1/2 tsp nutmeg            ⎪  electric mixer
1/4 tsp cloves            ⎭  bowl.

1/4 c butter or           ⎫  Add to dry ingredients.
  margarine, softened     ⎪  Blend quickly on low
1 c milk                  ⎬  speed to moisten. Beat
1 tsp vanilla             ⎭  on high speed for 1/2 min.
                             scraping bottom and sides
                             of bowl.
3 eggs - Add. Blend on low. Beat on med speed
         for 1 1/2 min longer.

Put into greased and floured pans.

Bake 350° 8" sq or 9" layers -30-40 min
     or 1 -13 x 9 oblong  40-45 min
Use a wooden pick to test.

# Creamy Penuche Icing

1/2 c butter or    - Melt in saucepan over
  margarine          med. heat.
1 c brown sugar,   - Add to melted butter. Cook
  packed             and stir until mixture bubbles.
                     Reduce heat. Cook and stir
                     2 min. longer.
1/4 c milk  - Add milk and blend. Return
              mixture to a boil, stirring
              continually. Remove from heat.
              Cool to lukewarm.

1 3/4 - 2 c        - Sift if lumpy. Add enough
  powdered sugar.    to make a frosting of
                     spreading consistency.

Frosts 2 layers or 1 - 13 x 9 cake.

# Orange Buttermilk Cake

350°                               (elec mixer)

## Single layer

1 1/2 c Baker's "Flower" ♥  
3/4 c sugar  
1/4 tsp baking soda  

} Stir together in smaller electric mixer bowl.

2 Tbsp butter or margarine, softened  
2/3 c buttermilk  
1 egg  
1 1/2 tsp grated orange peel  

} Add to dry ingredients Blend on low speed to moisten. Beat on high speed for 2 min scraping bottom and sides of bowl constantly.

Put into prepared pan - 8" sq or 9" round.
Bake 350° 30-35 min until top springs back when center is lightly touched.


## 2 layer or oblong pan

3 c Baker's "Flower" ♥  
1 1/2 c sugar  
1/2 tsp baking soda  

} Stir together in larger electric mixer bowl.

1/4 c butter or margarine, softened  
1 1/3 c buttermilk  
2 eggs  
1 Tbsp grated orange peel  

} Add to dry ingredients. Blend on low speed to moisten. Beat on high speed for 2½ min scraping bottom and sides of bowl.

Put batter into prepared 13 x 9 pan.
Bake 350° 35-45 min. (Or, bake in layers following pan size and baking time as for above single layer.

# Carrot Cake

350°                                     (elec. mixer)

1 1/3 c Baker's "Flower" ♥
1/2 c dk. brown sugar, packed
1/4 c sugar
1/2 tsp baking soda
1/2 tsp cinnamon
1/4 tsp nutmeg
} Stir dry ingredients together in smaller bowl of electric mixer.

1/2 c buttermilk - Add. Blend on low speed to moisten. Beat on med. speed for about 1 min.

2 eggs - Add. Blend and beat on med. speed for 1 more minute.

1 c shredded carrots (do not pack)
1/3 c chopped pecans
} Stir in carrots and nuts.

Put into a greased and floured 8" sq pan.

Bake 350° 30-35 min. Cake should spring back when touched lightly in the center.

# Cream Cheese Frosting

1 - 3 oz pkg cream cheese, softened
1 Tbsp butter or margarine, softened
} Whip together with a spoon or use mixer.

1 1/2 c powdered sugar
1 Tbsp milk
1/2 tsp vanilla
} Beat in, adding extra milk or powdered sugar if necessary. Stir until frosting is a smooth, spreading consistency.

Cool cake before frosting.

# Pound Cake

350°                                         (elec. mixer)

1¼ c Baker's "Flower" ♥  }  stir dry ingredients
½ c sugar                  together in smaller
¼ tsp nutmeg         elec mixer bowl.

2 Tbsp butter or       Add to dry ingredients.
  margarine, softened   Blend on low speed for
6 Tbsp milk            about 30 sec. Scrape
1 egg <u>plus</u> 2 egg yolks  bottom and sides of bowl,
½ tsp vanilla           while beating on med
                                 speed for about 2 min.

Put into a greased and floured loaf pan —
use either a 4 x 8 or 5 x 9.

Bake 350° 35-40 min. Let cool in pan for
about 10 min before removing cake.

Place cake on a cooling rack.

# Applesauce Cake

350°                                          (elec mixer)

2½ c Baker's "Flower" ♥ ⎫
1 ⅓ c sugar              ⎬ Stir together
½ tsp baking soda        ⎬ to blend.
½ tsp cinnamon           ⎪
¼ tsp nutmeg             ⎭

2 Tbsp butter or         ⎫  Add to dry ingredients.
  margarine, softened    ⎬  Blend on low to
2 eggs                   ⎪  moisten. Beat on med
1 c applesauce           ⎭  speed for about 2 min
                            while scraping bottom
                            and sides of bowl.

(⅔ c chopped nuts)  (stir in nuts)
Put into greased and floured pan or pans.
Bake 350° 11 x 8 - 35-40 min, 8" or 9" round
layers 30-35 min. or until wooden pick comes
out clean.
Cool. Dust with powdered sugar, if desired.

Variations:
Add ½ c chopped dates or raisins when
adding nuts.

Or, sprinkle unbaked batter with a mixture
of ½ c finely chopped nuts, 1½ Tbsp sugar, and
½ tsp nutmeg.

Substitute packed brown sugar or use half
(⅔ c) brown sugar and half (⅔ c) granulated.

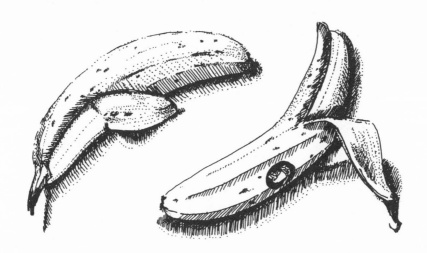

# Banana Nut Cake

350°                                     (elec. mixer)

2 c Baker's "Flower"   ⎫
1 c sugar   ⎬  Stir together in
½ tsp baking soda   ⎪  mixer bowl.
(dash of nutmeg)   ⎭

2 Tbsp butter or
   margarine, softened   ⎫  Add to dry ingredients.
½ c buttermilk   ⎬  Blend on low to moisten.
2 med-size, ripe   ⎪  Beat on med. speed
   bananas, mashed   ⎭  for about 1½ min.

2 eggs - Add eggs. Blend, then beat for
           1½ min longer.

½ c chopped nuts - Stir in nuts.

Put into a greased and floured 11"x 8" or
9" sq pan.

Bake 350° 35-45 min.

Cake is done when wooden pick comes
out clean and center springs back when
lightly touched.

Sprinkle with powdered sugar or frost with
an icing of your choice.

# Boston Cream Pie

350°                                     (elec. mixer)

1½ c Baker's "Flower" ♥ } Stir together in
3/4 c sugar            } smaller bowl of
                 electric mixer.

½ c milk
2 eggs, separated } Add milk, vanilla, and only
½ tsp vanilla      1 egg yolk. (Reserve other
                 yolk for CREAM FILLING)
                 Blend on low speed. Beat
                 on high for 2 min scraping
                 bottom and sides of bowl.

Beat egg whites separately until stiff but
not dry. Fold into batter.

Put into a greased and floured 8" or 9"
round layer pan.

Bake 350° 30-35 min. Cool in pan for
8-10 min before removing from pan to
cooling rack.

Cool. Split cake horizontally. Remove
top layer. Cover with CREAM FILLING.
Replace top half. Frost with CHOCOLATE
GLAZE or COCOA GLAZE. Refrigerate.

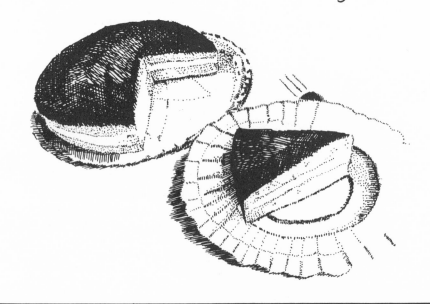

# Cream Filling

⅓ c Baker's "flower" ♥ } stir together in a
¼ c sugar } small bowl. Set aside.

1 egg yolk - Beat with a fork in a measuring
⅓ c milk     cup or small bowl. Mix ⅓ c milk
             with the egg yolk. Add this to the
             sugar-flour mixture. Blend.

1 c milk - Heat remaining 1 c milk to a near
           boil over med. heat.

Using a whisk, stir pudding mixture into the
hot milk. Continue stirring with the whisk
until the pudding has thickened and is
beginning to bubble.

Remove from heat. Press plastic wrap
directly onto pudding surface to prevent
drying as pudding cools.

# Boston Cream Pie Glazes

## CHOCOLATE GLAZE

1 sq unsweetened chocolate } Melt together over
1 Tbsp butter or margarine } low heat. Remove
                             from heat.

1 c powdered sugar       } Add to melted chocolate
1 tsp vanilla            } beginning with 2 Tbsp
2-3 Tbsp hottest tap water } hot water. Add more
                             if needed.

## COCOA GLAZE

1 c powdered sugar } Stir or sift until
3 Tbsp cocoa       } finely blended.

2 Tbsp butter or      }
  margarine, melted   } Add and stir until smooth.
2 Tbsp hot water      } Sparingly, add more water
½ tsp vanilla         } if the glaze is too thick.

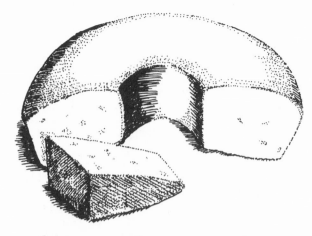

# Lemon Bundt Cake

350°                                        (elec mixer)

2 1/2 c Baker's "Flower" ♥  
1 1/3 c sugar  
1 pkg (3 3/4 oz) <u>instant</u> lemon pudding  
          } Measure into larger mixer bowl. Stir to blend.

2 Tbsp vegetable oil  
1 c milk  
      } Add. Blend on low speed to moisten. Beat on med speed scraping bottom and sides of bowl for 1 min.

4 eggs       Add eggs. Blend in at low speed. Beat 2 min longer on med, scraping bowl occasionally.

Put into a greased and floured bundt or tube pan - 9"-10" or a 13x9 pan.

Bake 350°    Bundt or tube   55-60 min  
              Oblong cake pan 40-45 min

Cool cake for 5 min before glazing.

## Lemon Glaze

1 1/2 c powdered sugar  
1/2 c lemon juice  
      } Add juice in several additions. Beat well after each.

Prick cake with fork tines. Drizzle lemon glaze over the cake.

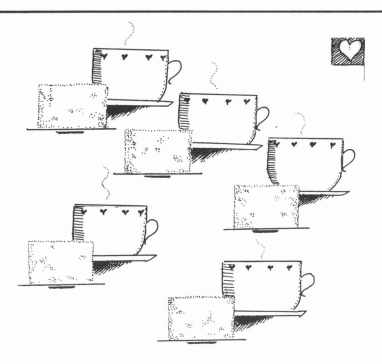

# Plain Vanilla Snack Cake

375°

1 Tbsp butter or
   margarine, softened } Use the back of a
   spoon to grease the
   bottom of an 8" sq cake pan.

1 1/3 Baker's "Flower" ♥ )
3/4 c sugar           )  Measure ingredients
1/2 c milk            )  and put in the
1 egg, beaten         )  cake pan. Using the
1 tsp vanilla         )  "greasing" spoon, mix
                         until well-blended.

<u>Bake 375°</u> 25-30 min. until wooden pick
comes out clean.

OPTIONS:
   Add 1/4 c chopped nuts to the batter.

   Add a handful of chocolate chips to batter.

   Sprinkle top of batter with sugar and
   cinnamon.— then bake.

   After baking, top with BROILER ICING —see
   BASIC CAKE VARIATIONS.

# Chocolate Snack Cake

375°

3 Tbsp vegetable oil – Measure into an 8" sq. or 9" round cake pan. Tilt to grease bottom.

1 c Baker's "Flower" ♥
1/4 c cocoa
2/3 c sugar
1/4 tsp baking soda
} Mix together in a separate bowl. Rub back of spoon against sides of bowl (or use fingertips) to make a smooth powdery mixture. Dump into cake pan.

1 egg – Beat egg in a glass measuring cup.
Water  – Add water to the 3/4 c mark.
1 tsp vanilla – Stir into the egg and water. Add to the dry ingredients.

Using a fork, stir until mixture is uniform. Bake 375° 25-30 min or until a wooden pick comes out clean. Let cool. Sprinkle with powdered sugar.

# Applesauce Snack Cake

1 Tbsp butter or margarine, softened
} Using the back of a teaspoon, spread butter over bottom of 8" sq. cake pan.

1 1/4 c Baker's "Flower" ♥
2/3 c sugar
1/2 tsp cinnamon
1/4 tsp nutmeg
} Stir together to blend. Dump into buttered pan.

1/2 c applesauce
1 egg, beaten
} Add to dry ingredients. Beat with a fork until well-blended.

2 tsp sugar
1/4 tsp nutmeg
1/4 c chopped nuts
} Mix together and sprinkle over unbaked cake.

Bake 375° 25-30 min or until wooden pick comes out clean.

Pies

# Pie Baking Tips & Information

Do not prick bottom crust <u>if</u> the filling is to be baked with the pastry.

Top crusts should have small openings made near the center to allow steam to escape.

Bottom and top crusts will seal better if edges are moistened with water, milk, or egg before the two are pressed together.

Oven-proof glass or darkened or dull finished aluminum <u>bake</u> with best results.

Bake pies in lower third of the oven.

To prevent over-browned edge on top crust, cover <u>partially baked</u> crust with aluminum foil. Tear off a square of foil, cut a 6" circle out of the center, crimp edges downward and place loosely over the pie. (See diagram below.)

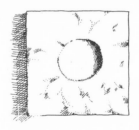 

## GLAZES FOR PIE-CRUSTS

<u>Shiny top crust</u> - Brush with mixture of 1 Tbsp milk and 1 tsp sugar before baking.

<u>Sugary top crust</u> - Brush with milk or water and sprinkle with sugar before baking.

<u>French egg wash</u> - Mix egg yolk or beaten egg with a little water. Brush over top crust before baking.

# Directions for Making Pie Pastries

Two pastry recipes are included in this section. The main difference is that the EASY·AS·PIE CRUST is made with milk. It is somewhat easier to handle and is a bit more generous in size. The STIR AND ROLL PASTRY is made with water and is slightly more fragile.

They are made in identical methods.

1. Combine liquids and dry ingredients. Stir till dough gathers and cleans sides of bowl.

2. Shape into a flattened round.

3. Roll between 2 sheets of waxed paper to 1/8" thickness. The bottom crust should be about 2½" larger than pan diameter.

4. Remove the top sheet of waxed paper. Sprinkle exposed pastry with a rounded teaspoonful of flour.

5. <u>Invert</u> (paper-side up) over pie pan. Gently peel off paper.

6. Ease pastry into pan. Trim and shape edge.

7. Prick generously with tines of fork for single crust.

8. If time allows, <u>refrigerate</u> to firm pastry. The crusts seem to hold their shape best when chilled before baking. (Be sure that your pie plate can go from refrigerator to oven).

9. If pastry "puffs" away from pan while baking, quickly and carefully, reach into oven and prick a few times.

10. Bake until lightly browned.

# Easy-as-Pie Crust

1 1/4 c flour
1/3 c Baker's "Flower" ♥   } Measure dry ingredients into mixing bowl. Stir to blend.
1/4 tsp salt

6 Tbsp vegetable Oil — Put oil into a glass measuring cup.

Milk
  (4 2/3 Tbsp) — Add milk to oil in measuring cup to the 2/3 c mark. Stir together with a fork.

Add all at once to the dry ingredients. Mix with fork until dough cleans sides of bowl.

To shape, refer to "directions for making pie pastries".

Bake 475° 12-15 min.

Variation: STONE·GROUND WHEAT PASTRY - Use 2/3 c flour plus 2/3 c stone·ground wheat flour. Follow above directions adding 1/3 c ♥ etc.

# Stir and Roll Pastry

1 c + 2 Tbsp flour
1/4 c Baker's "Flower" ♥ } Blend in mixing bowl
1/4 tsp salt

1/3 c vegetable oil - Measure into a glass (liquid)
measuring cup.

Water - Add to oil until it reaches the 1/2 c
mark (at eye level). Stir together.

Add all at once to dry ingredients. Stir quickly
just till dough begins to clean sides of bowl.
Gather and shape into a flattened round.

Roll between 2 sheets of waxed paper to a
12" diameter. Refer to "directions for making
pie pastries"

Bake 475° 12-15 min.


# Stir and Roll Pastry
# for a 2-crust Pie

2 1/4 c flour
1/2 c Baker's "Flower" ♥ } Blend well in a
1/2 tsp salt                  mixing bowl.

2/3 c vegetable oil - Measure oil into glass
measuring cup.

Water - Add to oil until it reaches the 1 c
mark (at eye level). Stir together.

Add all at once to dry ingredients, Stir quickly
just till dough begins to clean sides of bowl.
Gather and shape into 2 flattened rounds.

Bake as recipe directs.

# Cookie Crumb Crusts

For a 9" crust:

1½ c fine crumbs   } Mix together in a bowl.
3 Tbsp sugar

⅓ c butter or    – Add to crumbs. Toss
  margarine, melted   till well-blended.

Bake 375° – Cool thoroughly before filling.

(Or, do not bake but chill for 1 hour before filling).


For an 8" crust:

1¼ c fine crumbs } Mix together in a bowl.
2 Tbsp sugar

¼ c butter or    – Add; prepare as above.
  margarine, melted


For Cookie Crumbs:

Use store-bought cookies or any type of home-made cookie which can be crushed into <u>dry</u> crumbs —— such as graham crackers, sugar cookies, chocolate wafers, etc.

# Vanilla Cream Pie Filling

## (Basic Recipe)

3/4 c Baker's "Flower" ♥ } Stir together in a
2/3 c sugar } saucepan or top of
double boiler pan.

1/4 c milk - Add to mixture in pan. Blend.

3 egg yolks - Add. Use a whisk to blend
thoroughly.

2 1/2 c milk - "Whisk" milk in gradually. Cook
and stir with whisk until mixture
comes to a boil. Boil one minute
longer, stirring constantly. Remove
from heat.

1 tsp vanilla - Stir in the vanilla flavoring.

Pour hot filling into <u>baked</u> 9" pie shell.

Top with meringue, if desired.

# Vanilla Cream Filling for an 8" Pie Shell

1/2 c Baker's "Flower" ♥ } Stir together in saucepan
7 Tbsp sugar }

3 Tbsp milk - Stir in to form a "paste".

2 egg yolks - Add. Stir till well-blended.

1 3/4 c milk - Add gradually. Cook and stir
until mixture comes to a boil.
Cook 1 min longer.

1 tsp vanilla - Remove from heat. Stir in
vanilla flavoring.

Pour <u>hot</u> filling (unless directed otherwise) into
<u>baked</u> and <u>cooled</u> 8" pie shell.

# Variations of Cream Pie Filling

**COCONUT CREAM** – Add ½ c moist shredded coconut to Basic VANILLA CREAM PIE FILLING. Fold in just before filling the <u>baked</u> pie shell.

Add ¼ c coconut to meringue topping before baking. Or, toast shredded coconut and sprinkle over whipped cream topping.

**BANANA CREAM** – Make and <u>cool</u> Basic Cream pie filling before spooning half of it into a cooled baked pastry shell. Slice 1-2 bananas over the pudding. Spoon remaining vanilla pudding over the bananas. Top with whipped cream and more banana slices, if desired.

**PINEAPPLE CREAM** – Add well-drained crushed or cubed pineapple to filling. Use 3/4 c for a 9" pie and ½ c for an 8" pie. Add pineapple to the <u>hot</u> filling.

**BUTTERSCOTCH CREAM** – Substitute 1 c brown sugar for the granulated sugar. Use only 3/4 c for an 8" pie.

**CHOCOLATE CREAM** – Decrease ♥ to ½ c. Increase sugar to 3/4 c. Add 2 sq (2 oz) unsweetened chocolate with the milk. Cook and stir as for Basic Cream Pie Filling.

Or, add 1-6 oz pkg choc chips to the hot pudding. Stir to blend. Spoon into baked and cooled 9" pie shell.

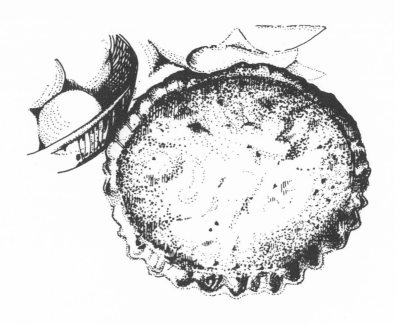

# French Apple Pie

6-7 c sliced apples } Toss gently to coat.
1 Tbsp lemon juice }

⅓ c light brown sugar,
  packed
⅓ c sugar
¼ c Baker's "flower" ♥ } Mix together.
1 tsp cinnamon
¼ tsp nutmeg

} Mix together.
Sprinkle over
prepared apples.
Stir carefully
to mix.

Put into unbaked 9" pie pastry. Sprinkle
with CRUMB TOPPING FOR FRUIT PIE.

Bake 400° 45-55 min in lower third of oven.
(Cover loosely with aluminum foil if top seems
to be browning too quickly).

APPLES FOR PIES — You'll need from 2-2½ lbs.
of tart, firm apples for a 9" pie. Use apples
such as Greenings, Jonathans, or any other
kind designated especially for pie baking.

# Crumb Topping for Fruit Pie

3/4 c flour
1/2 c brown sugar, packed } Stir to blend.
1/2 tsp cinnamon

1/3 c butter or } Add to dry mixture. Cut
margarine, firm } in until crumbly.

### * OR *

2/3 c flour
1/4 c Baker's "Flower" ♥ } Stir to blend.
1/3 c sugar

6 Tbsp butter or ) Add to dry mixture. Rub
margarine, firm ) together until well-blended
crumbs form.
(1/4 c chopped nuts)    ( Stir in nuts)

Sprinkle over fruit-filled pies. Pat lightly to
firm crumbs. Length of baking time will
depend on type of fruit.

For CANNED PIE FILLINGS — Put fruit into
a buttered 9" pie plate. Top with crumbs.
Bake 400° 25-30 min.

# Pumpkin Pie

½ c sugar
¼ c brown sugar
½ tsp salt
2 tsp cinnamon } stir together until
½ tsp nutmeg    well-blended.
¼ tsp ginger
¼ tsp cloves

2 eggs, slightly beaten   } Add to sugar-spice
1 c undiluted evaporated  } mixture. Beat
  milk                    } with spoon or
1-15 oz can pumpkin       } whisk to blend well.

1 - 9" unbaked pie shell  -  Pour into pie shell.

Bake 425° (lower 3rd of oven) for 15 min.
Reduce heat to 350° and bake 45 min longer—
or, until knife inserted near center comes
out clean.

# Rhubarb Custard Pie

4 c coarsely chopped    - Prepare and set
  rhubarb                 aside.

1 c sugar
1 Tbsp flour   } stir together in a
¼ tsp salt     } mixing bowl.
⅛ tsp nutmeg

2 eggs, slightly beaten } Add to the dry
2/3 c half and half     } mixture. Blend
  or evap. milk         } well with mixing
                        } spoon or whisk.

1 - 9" unbaked pie shell } Sprinkle flour evenly
1 Tbsp flour             } over bottom of pastry.
                         } Cover with rhubarb.

½ c sugar - sprinkle over the rhubarb.

Pour egg-milk mixture over the fruit.

Bake 350° - lower third of oven for about
1 hr or until knife comes out clean.

# Pecan Pie

3 eggs
2/3 c sugar
1/2 tsp salt
1/3 c butter or
  margarine, melted
1/2 c dark corn syrup
1/2 c light corn syrup

} Beat in a mixing bowl with a rotary beater.

1 c broken pecans - Add and stir into above mixture.

1 unbaked 9" pie shell - Pour into the pastry.

Bake 375°  40-50 min or until filling is set.

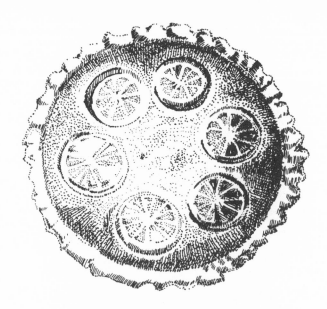

# Southern Lemon Pie

| | |
|---|---|
| 1 c sugar<br>1/4 c Baker's "Flower" ❤ | Rub together by pressing with back of spoon. |
| 4 eggs<br>1 c light corn syrup<br>1/4 c melted butter or margarine<br>1 tsp grated lemon rind<br>1/3 c lemon juice | Add to sugar-flour mixture. Beat with whisk or mixing spoon until well-blended. |

1 - 9" unbaked pie shell - Pour mixture into unbaked pastry.

Top with paper-thin lemon slices, if desired.

<u>Bake 375°</u> (lowest oven rack) for 45 min or until filling is golden brown.

Cool thoroughly before cutting.

<u>About LEMONS</u> — The amount of juice per lemon varies. 1 Lemon will yield from 1-3 Tbsp. A smooth skinned fruit will be more juicy. There will be 1-1½ tsp grated rind from each lemon.

# Citrus Pie

1/2 c water
1 pkg unflavored gelatin (1 Tbsp)
} Measure water into top double boiler pan. Sprinkle gelatin over the water. Let soften 5-10 min. Set pan over hot water. Heat to dissolve.

1 - 6 oz can citrus concentrate, thawed
} Put into blender container. Add dissolved gelatin.

1 can sweetened condensed milk
- Add milk gradually while blending on low speed.

2 egg whites
- In a separate bowl, beat whites to soft peak stage.

Fold the citrus mixture with the beaten whites.

Spoon into <u>baked</u> pastry shell or into a crumb crust. Refrigerate.

Top with whipped cream, if desired.

# Berries and Cream Pie

1/2 c Baker's "Flower" ♥
1/2 c sugar
1 tsp unflavored gelatin
} Stir together in a saucepan.

2 c milk - Add <u>3 Tbsp only</u> to mixture in saucepan. Stir to make a paste. Gradually add remaining milk.

Cook and stir over med. heat until pudding boils. Boil 1 min longer. Remove from heat. Press plastic wrap directly onto pudding surface. Cool until it begins to set. (Remove paper).

1 c whipping cream
1 tsp vanilla
- Beat cream until stiff. (add flavoring when partially beaten).

Fold half of the beaten whipped cream into the <u>cooled</u> pudding. Put into <u>baked</u> 8" or 9" pastry. Spoon remaining whipped cream over the top. Garnish with fresh berries.

# Brownie Fudge Pie

(no crust)

1 c sugar
½ c dry cocoa powder
⅓ c Baker's "flower" ♥
} Measure into mixing bowl. Using back of spoon, rub against bowl to blend and remove lumps.

½ c light corn syrup
3 Tbsp melted butter
} Add and mix well.

1 large can (13 oz) evaporated milk — Add milk gradually and blend thoroughly.

2 eggs, beaten — Add eggs. Stir to incorporate.

Pour into a well-buttered 9"-10" pie plate.

½ c chopped pecans — Sprinkle with nuts.

Bake <u>350°</u> for 40-45 min. The center will be soft but will firm as it sets.

Serve warm or cold with vanilla ice cream.

# No-Crust Pumpkin Pie

3/4 c sugar
1/2 c Baker's "Flower" ♥
2 tsp cinnamon
1/2 tsp nutmeg
1/4 tsp cloves
1/4 tsp ginger
— Stir together in a mixing bowl. Rub with spoon or fingers to remove lumps.

1 can (15-16 oz) pumpkin — Add to dry ingredients. Stir vigorously.

2 eggs, slightly beaten — Add. Beat with a whisk or mixing spoon to blend throughly with pumpkin mixture.

1 can (13 oz) evaporated milk — Add milk. Mix till well blended.

Pour into a buttered 9"-10" pie plate.

Bake 350° 50-65 min or until knife inserted near center comes out clean.

# Whipped Cream Topping

1 c whipping cream
2 Tbsp powdered sugar
1/2 tsp flavoring
— Using a rotary beater and chilled bowl, whip together until stiff.

Do not over-beat or the whipped cream will separate.

1 c whipping cream will make 2 c whipped cream.

Some recipes suggest that gelatin will help "hold up" whipped cream. Soften 1 tsp unflavored gelatin in 1 Tbsp water. Heat over hot water to dissolve. Add cooled dissolved gelatin to slightly thickened whipped cream. Continue beating until stiff.

# Traditional Meringue Topping

For a 9" pie:

3 egg whites } Beat together until
¼ tsp cream of tartar } frothy.

6 Tbsp sugar (or ½ - Add 1 Tbsp at a
   c powdered sugar)    time beating until
         stiff and glossy.

Pile onto hot filling. <u>Seal</u> to rim of crust.

Bake 375° for 10-12 min until lightly browned.


For an 8" pie:

2 egg whites } Beat
¼ tsp cream of tartar }

¼ c sugar (or 6 Tbsp } add
   powdered sugar

     and bake as above.

# Baker's Meringue for Pies

2 Tbsp sugar } Blend in a small saucepan.
1 Tbsp cornstarch }

½ c water - Add. Boil until clear, stirring
        constantly. <u>Set aside.</u> Cool to
        room temperature.

3 egg whites - Beat until foamy.

1 tsp lemon juice } Add to egg whites. Beat
pinch of salt    } to soft peak stage.

¼ c sugar - Gradually add sugar and beat
        thoroughly after each addition.
        Beat to firm glossy peaks.

Add cornstarch mixture. Fold in till thoroughly
blended. Spread over pie filling.

Bake 350° 12 min or until lightly browned.

# Other Desserts

# Apple Dumplings

| 6 sweet-tart med. sized baking apples | Slice across top of each apple. Peel, <u>or</u> leave peel on. Remove core. |
|---|---|

Make STIR-AND-ROLL PASTRY for a 2 crust pie – see PIE SECTION.

After mixing, gather into a ball. Flatten slightly. Cut into six wedges. Shape each piece of dough into a flattened square. Roll between 2 sheets of waxed paper to a 7"-8" square. Remove top sheet.

Place a cored apple in center of pastry square. (Fill cavity of apple with sugar-cinnamon mixture or a spoon of jelly, if desired.)

Use lower sheet of waxed paper to lift corners of pastry. Overlap pastry corners pressing to seal. Put into 13x9 pan – do not crowd. Place seam sides up or down.

Repeat with remaining apples.

Bake with SYRUP FOR APPLE DUMPLINGS or sprinkle with sugar. Put in a 425° oven and bake for 35-45 min or until golden brown. <u>Don't over-bake</u> – the apples may collapse!

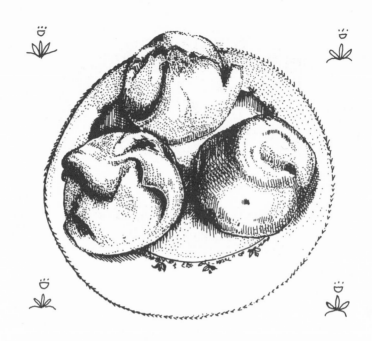

# Syrup for Apple Dumplings

(optional)

1 ½ c water  -  Heat in a saucepan.

1 c sugar
¼ tsp cinnamon
⅛ tsp nutmeg
3 Tbsp butter
} Add sugar, spices, and butter to the hot water. Stir until sugar dissolves.

Bring to a boil, stirring occasionally. Boil for about 4 min. Remove from heat.

Use about 1 Tbsp hot syrup to quickly glaze each apple dumpling. Carefully, pour remainder of syrup around the apples.

Or, make syrup. Do <u>not</u> bake with the apple dumplings. Boil down to desired consistency and serve on the side.

# Skillet Pie

1 2/3 c Baker's "Flower" ❤ } Blend together in
1 Tbsp sugar } a mixing bowl.

1/3 c milk } Add all at once. Stir
1 Tbsp butter or } until dough gathers.
margarine, melted }

Knead 10-15 turns on a lightly floured surface.

Shape into a ball. Flatten slightly and roll on a lightly floured board to about a 12" diameter. Dust top lightly with flour.

Carefully fold in half, then fold again. Lift and place point of dough in center of an 8"-9" oven-proof skillet (or equivalent-sized casserole dish). Dough may hang over edges — do not trim.

Fill with one of the following FRUIT FILLINGS FOR COBBLERS. Fold dough towards center leaving a space or cut steam vent if dough over-laps.

Bake 425° 25 min or until golden brown.

# Pastry for Danish Apple Bars

(prepare apple filling first)

2 1/4 c flour
1/2 c Baker's "Flower" ♥ } Blend together in a
1/2 tsp salt                    mixing bowl.

10 Tbsp vegetable oil   - Measure oil into glass
   (scant 2/3 c)          measuring cup (slightly
                          below the 2/3 c mark at
                          eye level.
water (1/3 c)            Add water to just slightly
                          below the 1 c mark

1 egg, <u>separated</u> - Add beaten egg yolk to water
(reserve white)          and oil. Stir to blend. Add
                          all at once to dry ingredients.

Stir quickly, just till dough begins to clean sides
of bowl. Gather together. Divide in half.

Shape each into a flattened rectangle. Roll
one at a time between 2 sheets of waxed
paper to fit a 15x10 jelly roll pan.

Remove top sheet of paper. Invert over pan.
Carefully remove 2nd sheet. Shape to fit.

1 1/2 c cornflakes - crush cereal and sprinkle
                      over pastry in jelly roll pan.

# Apple Filling

7-8 c thinly sliced  ⎫
   baking apples     ⎪
2/3 c sugar          ⎬ toss gently to coat
1/2 tsp cinnamon     ⎪ apples. Spoon evenly
1/4 tsp nutmeg       ⎭ over crushed flakes.

Roll remaining pastry half between waxed paper
as above. Shape pastry over apple filling.

Beat reserved egg white until soft peaks form.
Spread over the pastry.

Bake 350° 55-60 min or until golden brown.

# Frosting for Danish Apple Bars

1 c powdered sugar ⎫ Make a thin icing. Spread
½ tsp vanilla      ⎬ over __warm__ bars.
1 - 2 Tbsp water   ⎭

(3 Tbsp chopped nuts)  (Sprinkle with nuts)

Cut into 30 bars.

# Fruit Cobbler

(dropped)

1 ½ c Baker's "Flower" ♥ } Stir to blend in a
2 Tbsp sugar                      } mixing bowl.

½ c milk - Add milk all at once. Stir just
to blend. Drop 6 evenly spaced
spoonfuls on top of <u>hot</u> fruit
filling.

Bake 400° 25-30 min or until golden brown.


# Fruit Cobbler Pie

(rolled)

1 ½ c Baker's "Flower" ♥ } Blend together in
2 Tbsp sugar                      } a mixing bowl.

¼ c milk — Add. Stir till dough gathers.
Knead a few turns. Shape into
a flattened ball. Dust with flour.
Roll between 2 sheets of waxed
paper to about ¼" thick. Remove
top paper. <u>Invert</u> over filling.

Remove top paper carefully. Trim dough if
necessary. Shape edge as desired. Prick
well with fork or cut design as a steam
escape.

Bake 400° 25-30 min or until golden brown.

# Fruit Fillings for Cobblers

## FRESH PEACH

6 ripe peaches } toss peeled and sliced
1 tsp lemon juice } peaches with lemon juice.

1/2 c sugar
2 Tbsp Baker's "Flower" ♥ } Rub together. toss
1/4 tsp cinnamon } gently with peaches.

## FRESH BERRIES

Blueberry  -  Substitute about 4c fresh
berries for the peaches. Do
not add cinnamon. Follow same
directions.

Cherry  -  Use about 4 c fresh cherries.
Increase sugar to 1¼c. Replace
Baker's "Flower" with 3 Tbsp
cornstarch.

## CANNED FRUITS - Use about ¼ c sugar
mixed with 1 Tbsp cornstarch.
(Use only with
top crust type
cobblers)
Drain juice from fruit into
saucepan. Add sugar mixture
cook and stir till thickened.
Combine with fruit.

## CANNED FRUIT PIE FILLINGS

For DROPPED COBBLER, <u>heat</u> fillings in oven
while preparing the dough. The fillings must
be hot to bake dough thoroughly.

# Cobbler Crunch

350°

1 1/3 c Baker's "Flower" ♥ } stir together
3/4 c sugar                  to blend.

1/2 of a beaten egg
(about 2 Tbsp)        - Toss with dry
                       ingredients to form
                       a coarse crumb.

1 can (21 oz) fruit
pie filling        - Spread evenly in an
                    ungreased 9" pie plate.

Sprinkle the crumb mixture over filling.

Bake in middle of 350° oven for 40 min.


# Old-Fashioned Shortcake

450°

2 1/4 c Baker's "Flower" ♥ } Stir together in
2 Tbsp sugar               a mixing bowl.

1/2 c milk -Add all at once. Stir just till
              dough gathers.

Knead on a lightly floured board 10-12 turns.

Roll between 3/8" - 1/2" thickness. Cut with a
2"-2 1/2" floured biscuit cutter.

Place on ungreased baking sheet. Prick each
3 times with fork tines.

Brush tops with 1 Tbsp melted butter or
margarine.

Sprinkle lightly with sugar - use about 1/4 tsp
per biscuit.

Bake 450° 8-10 min.        Makes 10-15 biscuits

Split. Serve with fresh fruit and cream.

# Shortcake Biscuits

450°

2 c Baker's "Flower" ♥ } Stir together in
2 Tbsp sugar             } a mixing bowl.

1 egg - Beat egg in a glass measuring cup.

Milk or cream - Add to beaten egg until it
reaches the ½ c mark.

Pour all at once into dry ingredients. Stir
quickly to form a soft dough.

Turn onto lightly floured board and knead
15-20 times.

Divide into 2 parts. Shape into flattened
rounds.

Press into 2 greased 8" round layer pans

Brush each with 1 tsp melted butter. Sprinkle
with 1 tsp sugar. Prick with tines of fork.

Bake 450° 10-12 min.

# Easy Shortcake

2½ c Baker's "Flower" ♥ } Stir to blend in
2 Tbsp sugar             } a mixing bowl.

3/4 c milk - Add. Beat with mixing spoon
until blended. (Mixture will be
grainy).

Spread in 2 greased 8" round layer pans.

Bake 450° 12-15 min.

# Strawberry Shortcake

Prepare OLD-FASHIONED or EASY SHORTCAKE

Place 1 layer upside down on a serving plate.

> 1 qt. strawberries ⎫ Toss cleaned, sliced
> 1/2 c sugar ⎭ berries gently with
>   sugar.

Put <u>half</u> of the berries on the first layer.

Top with second layer, placing it right side up.

Cover with remaining berries (save a few whole berries for garnishing) and whipped cream.

> 1 c whipping cream ⎫ whip together in
> 2 Tbsp powdered sugar ⎭ a chilled bowl
>   until stiff.

# Apple Crisp

375°

4 c sliced cooking — Wash, pare, quarter
   apples                    and slice.
1/4 c sugar — Toss apples with sugar

Put into a greased 8" sq pan.

1/3 c sugar
1/3 c brown sugar, packed
3/4 c Baker's "Flower" ♥          combine in a
1/2 c quick rolled oats           mixing bowl.
3/4 tsp cinnamon
1/4 tsp nutmeg

1/4 c butter or        — Add to dry ingredients.
   margarine, softened  Cut in or rub together
                        to form a crumb mixture.
(1/4 c chopped nuts) (Mix in nuts) Sprinkle
the crumb mixture over the prepared apples.

Bake 375° - 30 min or until golden brown
and apples are tender when pierced with
a fork.

# Fruit Pizza

4 Layers - Crust, cream cheese, fruit & glaze

1.  1 c flour
    ¼ c Baker's "Flower" ♥       } Stir together in
    ¼ c powdered sugar          } a mixing bowl
                                } until blended.

    6 Tbsp butter or            } Add slightly cooled
    margarine, melted           } melted butter and
    2 Tbsp milk                 } milk to dry ingredients.

Mix to make a cookie-like dough. Pat evenly
onto an ungreased 12" pizza pan. Form a
slight ridge around the edge. Prick well.

Bake 350° 18·20 min or until golden brown.

# Topping for Fruit Pizza

2.  1 - 8 oz. pkg cream cheese, ⎫ Mix together.
        softened              ⎬ spread over
    ½ c sugar               ⎭ <u>cooled</u> crust.

3.  Ripe, but firm fruit     – Prepare fruit. Peel
       (3 med peaches or      and slice, if necessary.
       nectarines <u>or</u>          Place in concentric
       1 pt. strawberries     circles on cream
       <u>or</u> desired fruit)      cheese layer.

4.  2 Tbsp sugar     ⎫ Combine in a
    1 Tbsp cornstarch ⎭ small saucepan.

    ½ c orange juice  – Add juice and stir
                       to blend ingredients.

    ½ c red currant jelly
    (a dash of cinnamon)  – Add jelly. Cook
    <u>or</u>, use ½ c apple     and stir until
     jelly for a lighter    mixture thickens
     colored glaze.        and boils. Cook
                      2 min longer,
                      <u>Cool slightly</u>

spoon glaze over fresh fruit. Chill. Serve
with whipped cream or ice cream.

# Lemon Cheesecake

350°

1 1/2 c Baker's "Flower" ♥ } Stir together in a
3/4 c sugar             } mixing bowl. Remove
                          1/2 c. Set it aside.

1/4 tsp cinnamon - Add to dry ingredients in bowl. Blend

2 Tbsp beaten egg  -Beat 1 whole egg. Remove 2 Tbs
  (reserve remainder) and stir with oil. Mix with
                      dry ingredients.

Shape into a flattened round. Press into bottom
of a lightly greased 9-10" springform pan.

Bake 350° 12-15 min or until slightly browned.

Prepare filling below while crust bakes. (elec mixer)

2 - 8oz pkgs cream   - Beat in a large mixer bowl
  cheese, softened     until light and fluffy.

1/2 c sugar          } Add to the cream cheese
1 c dairy sour cream } along with the 1/2 c
2 eggs plus reserved } reserved dry ingredients.
  egg from crust.    } Blend on low speed.
2 Tbsp lemon juice   } Beat 2 min on med
1 tsp grated lemon rind} speed. Pour over baked
                       crust.

Bake 350° 35 min longer. Cool 15-20 min.

Top with :
  1 c dairy sour cream} Mix well. Spread
  1 1/2 Tbsp sugar    } over cheesecake.
  1/2 tsp vanilla     }

Return to 425° oven for 8 min. Cool to room
temperature. Refrigerate.

# Cheesecake Glazes

1 c fresh strawberries - wash, hull and mash to ½c.

¼ c sugar
1 Tbsp cornstarch } Blend together in saucepan.

2 tbsp water - Stir in water <u>and</u> <u>berries</u>.

Cook and stir until mixture thickens and boils. Cool. Spread over cheesecake.

<u>or</u>

1 - 10 oz box frozen strawberries, thawed  - Drain and reserve juice.

1 Tbsp sugar
1 Tbsp cornstarch } Blend in saucepan. Add juice. Cook and stir until thickened and clear. <u>Cool</u>.

stir in berries. Spread over cheesecake.

<u>or</u>

Melt jellies or preserves. Cool slightly before glazing cheesecake.

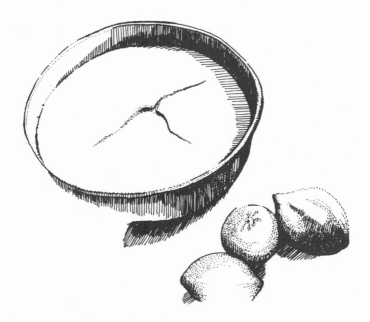

# Linzertorte

325°

| 1 c flour<br>1/4 c Baker's "Flower" ♥<br>1 Tbsp dry cocoa powder<br>1/2 tsp cinnamon | Stir together until blended. Set aside. |

| 1 c sugar<br>1/2 c butter or margarine, softened<br>1 egg<br>1 tsp grated lemon rind<br>1 c ground almonds (about 4 oz) | Stir vigorously in a separate bowl until well·mixed. Add dry ingredients. Stir again until thoroughly blended. |

Place 2/3 of the dough in a 9" springform pan. Shape to form a shell. Spoon an 8oz jar of apricot or raspberry jam over shaped dough.

Pipe remaining dough on to form a lattice-work top. Or, chill dough till firm and roll on a lightly floured board. Cut into strips or other designs as desired.

Bake 325° - 50 min.

Dust cooled torte with powdered sugar.

# Chocolate Sundae Cake

350°

1 ½ c Baker's "Flower" ♥ ⎫ Stir together in
3/4 c sugar          ⎬ a mixing bowl until
2 Tbsp dry cocoa     ⎭ well-blended.

6 Tbsp milk - Add to dry ingredients. Beat
with a mixing spoon to make
a smooth batter.

2 Tbsp milk ⎫ Add remaining milk and vanilla.
1 tsp vanilla ⎬ Mix thoroughly.

Spread batter in an 8" sq greased pan

½ c sugar           ⎫
½ c brown sugar ⎬ Blend dry ingredients.
⅓ c dry cocoa    ⎭ Sprinkle over batter.

1 ¼ c hottest tap water – Trickle over
the dry mixture.

Bake 350° 40-45 min.

# Baked Eggnog Custard

3 eggs      -      In a mixing bowl, beat eggs
with rotary (hand) beater. (Or,
use blender).

½ c sugar             ⎫ Add to eggs. Beat well.
¼ c Baker's "Flower" ♥ ⎭

1 large can (13 oz)    ⎫ Add evaporated milk,
   evaporated milk     ⎪ regular milk, and
2/3 c milk           ⎬ flavoring.
½ tsp vanilla        ⎪ Blend thoroughly.
¼ tsp lemon extract ⎭

Pour into buttered 1 ½ qt casserole dish (or
6 custard cups). Set in a larger pan. Fill
outer pan with about 1" hottest tap water.

Dust top of custard with nutmeg.

Bake 350° 45-50 min or until knife inserted
1" from edge comes out clean.

# Lemon Pudding Cake

350°

1 c sugar
1/2 c Baker's "Flower" ❤  } In a mixing bowl, stir to blend.

1/4 c water - Add. Stir vigorously until smooth.

3/4 c milk
Grated rind of 1 lemon } stir into the batter.

2 egg yolks - In a separate small bowl, beat until thick and lemon-colored.

1/3 c lemon juice - Mix with beaten yolks. Add and blend with batter.

2 egg whites - In a clean bowl, beat whites until almost stiff.

"Fold" the beaten whites into the batter.

Pour into a 1 qt buttered baking dish (or 6 custard cups)

Bake 350° 45-50 min or until brown on top.

# Vanilla Pudding

¼ c Baker's "Flower" ♥  } Blend together
¼ c sugar                } in a saucepan.

1 egg yolk  - Beat egg yolk in a 2 c glass
               measuring cup or a small bowl.

1½ c milk  - Add milk to egg yolk, stir
               to blend.

Blend 2 Tbsp of the milk-egg mixture
into the dry ingredients to make a paste.
Gradually add remaining liquid

Cook and stir over med heat until mixture
comes to a boil. Cook and stir 1 min
longer. (Use a whisk for stirring).

Remove from heat. Stir in ½ tsp vanilla.
Press plastic wrap directly onto hot pudding
to prevent a dried surface.

Variation:

# Chocolate Pudding

Add 3 Tbsp cocoa to dry ingredients and
increase sugar to ⅓ c. Use 3-4 Tbsp milk-
egg mixture to make a paste. Proceed as above.

# Pudding Ice Cream

1/3 c Baker's "Flower" ♥  
3/4 c sugar } Blend in saucepan.

2 c milk - Add 1/4 c only to the dry ingredients.  
   Stir to make a paste. Gradually  
   blend in the remaining 1 3/4 c milk.

Cook and stir over med heat until mixture comes to a boil. Remove from heat.

Press plastic wrap onto pudding surface. Cool. (Set pan in cold water to hasten cooling).

Put into a tray or shallow pan. Freeze for 1/2 hour, Turn cold mixture into a bowl and beat slightly.

1/2 c whipping cream - Beat until stiff.  
   Blend into chilled  
   mixture.

Return to freezer tray for 1 more hour. Beat again. Freeze 3-4 hours longer.

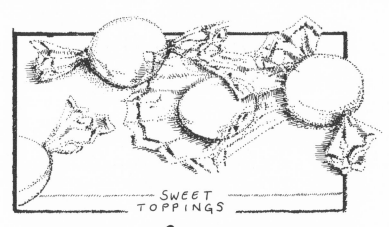

SWEET
TOPPINGS

# Butterscotch Sundae Sauce

1 1/4 c milk
1/4 c Baker's "Flower" ♥
1/4 c corn syrup
}
Blend together in
a saucepan. Cook
and stir until thick
and bubbly. Cook
2 min longer.
Remove from heat.

1 c dark brown sugar,
  packed
2 Tbsp butter
1/2 tsp vanilla
}
Stir into <u>hot</u> mixture.

Serve warm or cold over ice cream.
Refrigerate

# Chocolate Sundae Sauce

1 c sugar
1/3 c cocoa (dry)
3 Tbsp Baker's "Flower" ♥
}
Blend well in a
med-sized saucepan.

3/4 c milk - Add gradually to cocoa mixture.
         Stir well after each addition.

2 Tbsp butter
2 Tbsp light
  corn syrup
}
Add. Cook and stir over med
heat until mixture comes to a
boil. Cook 3-4 min longer.

About 1 1/2 c

# Ice Cream Sandwiches

350°

½ c brown sugar, packed
1 egg white, unbeaten
2 Tbsp butter or margarine, softened
1 tsp vanilla
} Beat together with a large mixing spoon.

⅔ c Baker's "Flower" ♥
¼ c dry cocoa
} Blend. Add to above mixture and beat well.

½ c flour - Stir in to make a very stiff dough. Knead by hand if necessary.
Shape into a flattened log. Place on a greased 16x14 <u>rimless</u> cookie sheet.

Cover with a large sheet of waxed paper. Using a rolling pin, flatten to about ⅛" thick. Carefully remove paper.

Cut into 2½" - 3" squares with a pizza cutter. Prick each square 3 times with fork tines.

Bake 350° 8-10 min. Let set a couple of minutes before removing to cooling rack. Cool thoroughly before filling with ice cream.

Cut a block of ice cream about ⅝" thick to fit cookies. Wrap each in foil. Freeze.

# Index